REPORT TO CONGRESS | December 2013

USAID Health-Related Research and Development Progress Report

**An Update of the 2011–2015
Health Research Strategy**

Preface

Ending preventable child and maternal deaths and creating an AIDS-free generation is within our reach. Modern-day science, technology and innovation, and the sharing of that knowledge, have allowed the global health community to accelerate progress toward these goals with hope and excitement.

In his 2013 State of the Union address, President Obama called upon Americans to join with the world to end extreme poverty in the next two decades. The U.S. Agency for International Development's (USAID's) contribution to this inspiring and reachable vision includes, in large part, our work in Global Health. Health-related research and development investments are foundational in ending preventable child and maternal deaths and creating an AIDS-free generation — all vital components of a healthier, more educated and peaceful world. Today, we have new tools, knowledge and expertise to achieve these goals, which were simply unimaginable in the past. It is in this context that I am pleased to share the *2013 Report to Congress: Health-Related Research and Development Progress Report.*

The 2013 Health-Related Research Report to Congress provides an update, broken down by health area, on the Agency's work under its multiyear strategy for health-related research and development. It reflects increased focus on implementation science, behavior change, health systems and the integration of health delivery services by sector.

USAID invests in research that pushes boundaries, advances health innovation and uses disruptive technologies to accelerate progress. These principles direct our work to address pressing health challenges that include malaria, tuberculosis, HIV and AIDS and other infectious diseases, as well as family planning and child and maternal survival. Keeping in mind that research is only as good as the ways in which we share knowledge and apply it to programs, USAID adheres to a managed "research-to-use" strategy. The Agency works to find ways to rapidly implement solutions and encourage our partners, including host countries, to adopt proven innovative approaches and technologies.

USAID's research portfolio demonstrates its commitment to evidence-based policies. Since 2011, USAID and partners have hosted four Evidence Summits that convened leading scholars and health practitioners to review the latest research in order to develop guidance for improved health performance, identify remaining knowledge gaps and formulate recommendations for research. The ultimate goal is to improve health policies, programs and research in low- and middle-income countries. Already, these summits have helped to address some key topics in global health, such as enhancing the provision and use of maternal health services through financial incentives, protecting children outside of family care, community and formal health system support for enhanced community health worker performance and a Population-Level Behavior Change Evidence Summit for Child Survival.

I am pleased to announce that USAID has partnered with Johns Hopkins and George Washington Universities to launch an open-access, peer-reviewed journal called *Global Health: Science & Practice.* The journal aims to enable the sharing of best practices and help in overcoming barriers to implementation. It does so by enhancing health practitioners and researchers' understanding of both the "what" and "how" of implementation.

USAID is about solutions, and the following report demonstrates our focus on how global health research and development contribute to the achievement of the U.S. Government's higher-level goals. We invite you to review this status report, and we thank Congress and the American people for their generosity and continued support.

Ariel Pablos-Méndez
Assistant Administrator

Table of Contents

Acronyms and Abbreviations

ACT	Artemisinin-based combination therapy
AMTSL	Active management of the third stage of labor
ART	Antiretroviral therapy
CAPRISA	Centre for the AIDS Programme of Research in South Africa
CBT	Compartmentalized Bag Test
CDC	Centers for Disease Control and Prevention
CHW	Community health worker
CHX	Chlorhexidine
CMAM	Community-based management of acute malnutrition
CSHGP	Child Survival and Health Grants Program
DOD	Department of Defense
DST	Drug sensitivity testing
EHFP	Enhanced Homestead Food Production
EONC	Essential obstetric and newborn care
FACTS	Follow-on African Consortium for Tenofovir Studies
FY	Fiscal year
GBV	Gender-based violence
GPP	Good Participatory Practice
GREAT	Gender Roles, Equality and Transformation
GSK	GlaxoSmithKline
HBB	Helping Babies Breathe
HRH	Human resources of health
HSS	Health systems strengthening
IAVI	International AIDS Vaccine Initiative
iCCM	Integrated community case management
IPTp	Intermittent preventive treatment for pregnant women
IRS	Indoor residual spraying
ITN	Insecticide-treated net
LAM	Lactational Amenorrhea Method
LPA	Line probe assay
MDR-TB	Multidrug-resistant TB
MgSO4	Magnesium sulfate
MMV	Medicines for Malaria Venture
MVDP	Malaria Vaccine Development Program
NIH	National Institutes of Health
ORS	Oral rehydration solution
PBF	Performance-based financing
PEER	Partnerships for Enhanced Engagement in Research
PEPFAR	U.S. President's Emergency Plan for AIDS Relief
PMI	President's Malaria Initiative
PMTCT	Prevention of mother-to-child transmission of HIV
PPH	Postpartum hemorrhage
QI	Quality improvement
R2P	Research to prevention
SARS	Severe acute respiratory syndrome
SEAD	Social Entrepreneurship Accelerator at Duke
STREAM	Standardised Treatment Regimen of Anti-Tuberculosis Drugs for Patients with MDR-TB
TB	Tuberculosis
UHC	Universal health coverage
UNICEF	United Nations Children's Fund
USAID	U.S. Agency for International Development
VCT	Voluntary counseling and testing
WHO	World Health Organization

EXECUTIVE SUMMARY

Many of the most significant achievements in human progress have come from harnessing the power of science, technology and innovation to accelerate economic development. At various points in our nation's history, 85 percent of global gross domestic product growth could be attributed to improvements made through science, technology and innovation.[1] In health, new and better ways are being developed to deliver low-cost, high-impact health interventions capable of reaching more people, saving more lives and lowering costs. Through simple, innovative and cost-effective solutions, the U.S. Agency for International Development (USAID) is helping to promote health in settings across the world.

USAID's global health research and development portfolio includes investments in more than 100 technologies in various stages of development. Several of these technologies are expected to be launched within the next 3 years. As these global health research products are developed, further research must inform how best they can be put into use in developing countries. Selected highlights of this year's research and development activities include:

- Validating a simplified approach to manage the third stage of labor that will enable lower-level skilled birth attendants to properly manage 66 percent of poor contractions of the uterus, a cause of hemorrhage and death. This advance promises to reduce the cost and complexity of training and make this lifesaving intervention more widely available.

- Demonstrating through evaluative research the efficacy of training lower-level health professionals to manage asphyxia, a leading cause of newborn mortality. USAID, through a public-private partnership, is supporting early introduction of this approach in 24 partner countries by rolling out training and implementation research.

- Developing and introducing chlorhexidine (CHX) antiseptic for umbilical cord care — a new, low-cost preventive intervention to reduce newborn infection, which causes up to 24 percent of newborn mortality. This is the second research product USAID has guided through a managed research-to-use process. The first product, oral rehydration solution and zinc, has been introduced as a treatment for diarrheal diseases in more than 20 USAID-supported countries. Product introduction for CHX is anticipated in at least 10 countries by 2016.

- Stimulating new approaches to support innovation. In partnership with Canada, the United Kingdom, Norway and the Bill & Melinda Gates Foundation, *Saving Lives at Birth: A Grand Challenge for Development* promotes disruptive technology development and helps drive innovative solutions.

- Expanding contraceptive options through the development of a multipurpose diaphragm. The SILCS diaphragm is a cervical barrier method that does not require a pelvic exam, is reusable and can potentially protect against HIV and sexually transmitted infections when paired with microbicide gels.

- Accelerating progress on HIV vaccine research by analyzing antibodies that neutralize a broad spectrum of HIV. The first three antigen candidates were placed into early product development. Research will potentially direct new vaccine designs by increasing our understanding of how these powerful proteins can block HIV.

- Developing the first-ever scientifically based prediction tool of unknown viruses that are potential candidate sources for emerging pandemic threats.

- Advancing from proof of concept, a prototype of a portable device for detecting counterfeit and substandard medicines. This device is less expensive and more accurate than current technologies. Using

it better ensures the availability of effective medicines and addresses a critical and increasingly recognized quality gap.

Rational scientific research will continue to inform the evidence-based decisions that guide the Agency's continued success.

The work highlighted in this report reflects USAID's engagement with multiple partners. USAID does not work in isolation; rather the Agency actively collaborates with the Centers for Disease Control and Prevention, the National Institutes of Health, the Department of Defense, multilateral and donor agencies, foundations, partner country governments, universities, nongovernmental organizations and private sector partners.

With strong support from the U.S. Presidential Administration and Congress, USAID is looking to science and technology to bring new solutions to existing challenges as the Agency continues to apply novel technical tools to diminish barriers and build partnerships to advance health around the world. These efforts help to discover the most efficient and sustainable means to ensure healthy, productive populations in developing countries, which are aligned with U.S. goals to end extreme poverty and promote peace and prosperity worldwide. The fulfillment of these goals will improve security at home and enhance markets for U.S. businesses abroad.

---

1 Committee on Science, Engineering and Public Policy. 2007. Rising Above the Gathering Storm: Energizing and Employing America for a Brighter Economic Future. National Academies Press.

MATERNAL AND NEWBORN HEALTH

BACKGROUND

The health of a mother throughout her pregnancy, during delivery and postpartum is directly linked to the health of her newborn. It is also connected in complex ways to the health of her whole family. In the United States, about 700 women a year die from preventable complications in pregnancy. Globally, however, the number is approximately 287,000. Seventy-nine percent of these maternal deaths occur in sub-Saharan Africa and South Asia, which are regions that also shoulder a heavy burden of deaths of children under the age of 5. Of the 6.6 million annual deaths of children under the age of 5, an estimated 2.9 million happen during the neonatal period.

Mothers and newborns are dying from preventable causes. Postpartum hemorrhage (PPH) (excessive bleeding after delivery), pre-eclampsia and eclampsia (high blood pressure during pregnancy) and sepsis (infection) are the leading direct causes of maternal mortality. The leading direct causes of neonatal mortality include sepsis, preterm births, asphyxia (lack of breathing) and congenital abnormalities.

The U.S. Agency for International Development (USAID), as part of the global health community, knows what works and how to address these easy-to-solve problems so that no mother loses her life while giving life and no child dies while coming into the world. More accurate data now exist for focus areas in maternal, newborn and child health to inform decisions around resource allocations, the strengthening of frontline service delivery, lifesaving commodities and behavior change. USAID and its global health partners have helped to decrease maternal deaths by nearly 50 percent since 1990. We have supported research and development activities to reduce maternal mortality as well as to advance newborn survival. For maternal health, our priorities include ensuring respectful quality care during pregnancy and birth, early prevention of maternal complications and access to high-quality drugs and services for pre-eclampsia and eclampsia and PPH. USAID is supporting efforts to advance the quality of newborn care through research and introduction activities. These activities aim to treat neonatal infections, manage newborn asphyxia and increase access to care.

Maternal Health

RESEARCH AND INTRODUCTION AREAS

Emergency obstetric care

The best treatment of postpartum hemorrhage is a class of drugs known as uterotonics, which include misoprostol and oxytocin; both are considered priority drugs by the U.N. Commission on Life-Saving Commodities. USAID is investigating whether drug quality issues, such as storage practices and product shelf life, limit how well these drugs work. The Agency is also researching business models on how to incentivize production, introduction, distribution and appropriate use.

Similarly, to address pre-eclampsia and eclampsia, USAID is developing business models to investigate the barriers to availability of and to facilitate use of magnesium sulfate (MgSO4), a low-cost treatment to manage pregnancy-related seizures. Health providers have cited one significant barrier related to use of MgSO4: dosage complexity and, in turn, fear of overdosing a patient. USAID is evaluating a single MgSO4 formulation as a solution and will collaborate with the World Health Organization (WHO) and manufacturers to advance this work in the coming year. If successful, this effort will significantly increase the uptake and regular use of this lifesaving treatment.

Active management of the third stage of labor (AMTSL) is a feasible, low-cost intervention to prevent approximately 66 percent of poor contractions of the uterus after birth, a cause of hemorrhage and death. AMTSL involves the administering of uterotonics (medication to help contraction of the uterus), controlled umbilical cord traction to deliver the placenta and uterine massage to prevent severe blood loss. WHO endorses AMTSL as a critical way to prevent PPH and reduce maternal mortality.

In a USAID/WHO study of eight countries, comparisons were made between standard AMTSL and a simplified version that excludes controlled cord traction. The study found that, compared with the full AMTSL package, the simplified approach had little additional risk of severe hemorrhage – 2.06 percent versus 1.88 percent. These research results are important because simplified AMTSL will reduce the complexity of the training for lower-level health professionals, and it will facilitate the wider use of AMTSL.

Another issue pregnant women face during emergency obstetric care is disrespect and abuse in health facilities. USAID is addressing these issues using implementation science. Preliminary results from Tanzania found that women who delivered in health facilities commonly experience verbal abuse, discrimination and abandonment of care. Early results from Kenya showed that abandonment, weak oversight, social norms and provider-client power dynamics contribute to disrespect, humiliation and abuse of pregnant women. This ongoing research will develop measures of their prevalence and evaluate potential interventions. Even before this work has been completed, it is already capturing the attention of researchers, health advocates, WHO and many others around the world.

Fistula

Obstetric fistula is a condition in which an abnormal opening or fistula forms in the birth canal. This maternal complication can be the result of prolonged, obstructed labor. It is particularly likely to occur when appropriate emergency obstetric care is not available – and it may lead to severe lifelong disabilities.

A five-country study concluded that existing fistula classification systems do not accurately predict fistula closure after surgery. This reinforced the need for consensus about clinical definitions and an evidence-based classification system to predict surgery outcomes. This study also documented the experiences that had led to women's fistula formation and women's quality of life while living with fistula and 3 months post-repair. The results highlight the supportive role that husbands, partners and families can play when women prepare for delivery. USAID, in partnership with WHO, is conducting an eight-country study in Africa comparing the efficacy and safety of 7-day catheterization with 14-day catheterization as a method to repair fistula. The shorter treatment has the potential to lower costs by reducing hospital stays.

Newborn Health

RESEARCH AND INTRODUCTION AREAS
Birth asphyxia
The Helping Babies Breathe (HBB) program, a USAID public-private partnership, is teaching resuscitation techniques to birth attendants to reduce the amount of preventable deaths from birth asphyxia. The program is currently in early introduction stage in 24 USAID partner countries. As part of implementation research in Kenya and Bangladesh, the program successfully showed that trained health professionals could recognize asphyxia and use high-quality resuscitation devices to treat it. Asphyxia-related neonatal deaths were reduced by 50 percent through implementing the HBB training program. In Malawi and Bangladesh, USAID is assessing the quality and coverage of programs to prevent neonatal deaths. The study will help key policymakers decide the utility of integrating HBB into basic obstetric and neonatal care.

USAID supports technology development to improve resuscitation devices that are low cost, high quality and simple to use. A recently completed study found that an upright neonatal resuscitator outperformed a standard resuscitator by delivering more volume, preventing air leakage and adopting a simpler assembly and disassembly for cleaning. USAID will undertake feasibility research in India as well as an assessment of market demand to take this technology development to the next stage of development.

Newborn sepsis prevention and treatment
Chlorhexidine (CHX) is a low-cost antiseptic that, when applied after birth to a newborn's umbilical cord, can prevent neonatal infections. Research and development supported by USAID in Bangladesh, Nepal and Pakistan showed that CHX reduced neonatal mortality by up to 23 percent. As part of this work, the Agency evaluated feasible delivery approaches and developed liquid and lotion versions of the product in anticipation of use. USAID is collaborating

with partner countries, the U.N. Commodities Commission and other technical assistance groups and manufacturers to develop, distribute and introduce CHX. Beginning with Nepal, which is already moving to national scale-up, CHX will be introduced in at least 10 countries by 2016. This effort illustrates USAID's managed research-to-use process to accelerate the availability and use of lifesaving products.

In partnership with the Bill & Melinda Gates Foundation's (Gates Foundation's) Saving Newborn Lives program and WHO, the Agency will complete a study comparing short-course antibiotic treatments for newborn sepsis with the WHO standard recommendation of hospitalization for 10 to 14 days, which is costly and not feasible in low-resource settings.

The simplified short-course treatments involve either fewer injections or switching treatment from injectable to oral antibiotics. If proven efficacious through this study, the new treatments would allow newborn sepsis care to be provided in lower-level health facilities on an outpatient basis or even outside health facilities. The ability to extend care to such settings is particularly important in areas where access barriers preclude hospitalization and newborns are not receiving appropriate care. This research is jointly supported by the Gates Foundation in Bangladesh and Pakistan and is complemented by a Gates Foundation and WHO study in three African countries. A WHO evidence review and, potentially, a new global recommendation are anticipated within the year. USAID is working with other partners, including the U.N. Commodities Commission, to address supply and other constraints to introduction. This new treatment approach promises to reach more sick newborns whose mothers do not currently access care and to reduce exposure to hospital-based pathogens and the cost of care.

Integrated Maternal and Newborn Health

RESEARCH AND INTRODUCTION AREAS
Evaluation of integration
Implementation of integrated approaches across maternal and newborn health and other services, such as nutrition and HIV and AIDS, holds promise to reduce mortality and increase efficiencies. If integration is

implemented poorly, it could distort service delivery systems, resulting in higher costs and inadequate services.

USAID is currently evaluating an integrated prevention of mother-to-child transmission of HIV health package in Tanzania to ensure that pregnant HIV-positive and HIV-negative mothers and newborns receive necessary services. The program, which is currently under evaluation, links communities to health facilities. These health facilities then deliver the integrated package of services, with support from community health workers. The preliminary midterm findings showed that a large proportion of women make their first visit to facilities far later than what is optimal. So USAID began to explore why significant numbers of HIV-negative and HIV-positive women are dropping out of the health system and are not accessing services at different points across the continuum of care (i.e., from the beginning of the antenatal period through the postnatal period). USAID's findings reinforce the importance of extension workers who can help link patients with health services. The findings also identified a need to focus more on improving facility quality, including the availability of drugs and test kits, reduction of wait times and improving client interaction.

Financing and incentives
Out-of-pocket costs prove to be a barrier for mothers who seek access to maternal and newborn care services. USAID is investing in innovative ways to encourage women to financially prepare for antenatal, delivery and postnatal care in low-resource settings. In Kenya, the Agency is evaluating a savings program in which women use mobile phones to regularly make small money transfers. Women can then use their saved balances to pay for critical maternal and newborn services. Using recent experiences from patients and providers in four hospitals, the evaluation will analyze whether the intervention alleviates the financial burden of health care and encourages women's babies to be delivered by trained health providers.

Maternal and newborn health services should not only provide appropriate coverage, but also they should achieve quality in performance. USAID evaluative research studies in Malawi and Senegal are examining the impact of performance-based financing (PBF), with special reference to measuring the interaction with the quality essential obstetric and newborn care that is delivered. This focus on quality issues as it relates to PBF has received limited attention in previous evaluative efforts and is a critical component to advance the sustainability of an approach that shows promise in getting women to deliver in health facilities. In fact, this issue was explored in the U.S. Government Evidence Summit on Maternal Health and Financial Incentives, a meeting that brought together global experts to advise on effective use of financial incentives to promote maternal health.

MEASUREMENT

WHO recently completed a 29-country study to characterize severe maternal morbidity and its management in health facilities. The USAID-supported study concluded that, while there was high coverage of essential maternal health interventions, such as MgSO4 for pre-eclampsia and eclampsia, coverage did not translate into mortality reduction. For example, in the deliveries that resulted in deaths or near misses in facilities, 18 percent of women did not receive any essential maternal interventions. These results stress the need for more attention on comprehensive emergency care (treatment of shock, surgery and advanced medical management) and on quality improvements to reduce maternal complications.

Complementing this global study, USAID assessed the quality of care in health facilities in Kenya, Tanzania, Mozambique and Madagascar and will complete this year's data collection in the Democratic Republic of the Congo. Early results from the assessments are guiding quality improvement and serving as the foundation for the development of low-cost proxy indicators of quality, such as those related to pre-eclampsia/eclampsia and postpartum hemorrhage. A related study in Mozambique detected that women were able to accurately report on several maternal and newborn health behaviors, including having a labor companion and placing the newborn skin-to-skin after birth. These results will be incorporated for use in regular household surveys and will be used to guide future program planning.

CHILD HEALTH

BACKGROUND

With 6.6 million children dying before the age of 5, USAID has targeted the major drivers of child deaths. Two conditions, namely pneumonia and diarrhea, account for roughly 30 percent of all deaths. The other major drivers of child deaths, malaria and newborn conditions, are addressed elsewhere in this report. In June 2012, the Child Survival *Call to Action*, convened by USAID, the United Nations Children's Fund (UNICEF), and the Governments of India and Ethiopia, highlighted the point that progress could be accelerated by applying what we already know, but it would require some strategic shifts in the way we do business. In recent years, implementation research has shown USAID how to carry out interventions for the prevention and

This research supports USAID's commitment to reduce child health deaths and aligns with key global initiatives, including A Promise Renewed, the Global Action Plan for Pneumonia and Diarrhea and the U.N. Commission on Life-Saving Commodities.

RESEARCH AND INTRODUCTION AREAS

Health provider engagement and family demand for treatment

Global guidelines recommend the use of oral rehydration solution (ORS) and zinc for diarrhea and dispersible amoxicillin for pneumonia. In many countries, however, these low-cost medications, particularly zinc and amoxicillin, are neither commonly recommended by providers nor used by the majority of families for these conditions.

between prescription knowledge and prescription behavior, while the intervention increased diarrhea treatment knowledge, it did not significantly result in an increase of sellers prescribing the recommended treatment.

Separate research in Uganda and Benin helped to address the barriers to uptake of ORS and zinc using interviews of providers and caregivers of children. The studies showed that, despite availability of zinc, inappropriate treatment recommendations by providers and lack of use by consumers continue to hinder progress in improving diarrhea case management.

Analyses of market research in a number of countries with high pneumonia burden are helping to better define provider and institutional behaviors, particularly in the private sector, around amoxicillin supply and demand. These studies will better refine future research and program strategies to address care-seeking and provider roles with these key commodities.

Uptake of integrated community case management

In developing countries, where many families find it difficult to reach health facilities quickly for child illness treatment, community health workers can be trained to effectively deliver services through integrated community case management (iCCM) for pneumonia, diarrhea and malaria where it is endemic. Recent scientific work on iCCM, supported by USAID and others, has been summarized in the November 2012 *American Journal of Tropical Medicine and Hygiene* supplement. The bottlenecks to iCCM use depend on each country's stage of iCCM implementation (e.g., introduction or scale-up of a new program versus refinement of an established program). USAID is funding ongoing studies that investigate the best approaches to help countries overcome the barriers that limit iCCM implementation in both the public and private sectors.

Implementation research activities are helping to better define how iCCM can be implemented most effectively and ef-

USAID-SUPPORTED RESEARCH ON DIARRHEA AND PNEUMONIA INTERVENTIONS

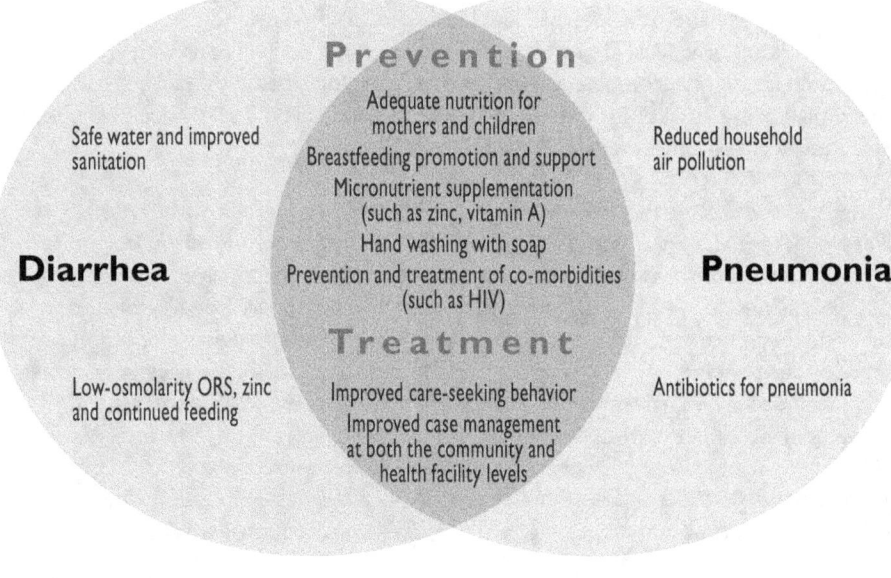

Prevention

Safe water and improved sanitation

Adequate nutrition for mothers and children
Breastfeeding promotion and support
Micronutrient supplementation (such as zinc, vitamin A)
Hand washing with soap
Prevention and treatment of co-morbidities (such as HIV)

Reduced household air pollution

Diarrhea

Pneumonia

Treatment

Low-osmolarity ORS, zinc and continued feeding

Improved care-seeking behavior
Improved case management at both the community and health facility levels

Antibiotics for pneumonia

Adapted from UNICEF Pneumonia and Diarrhea: Tackling the Deadliest Diseases for the World's Poorest Children, June 2012

treatment of pneumonia and diarrhea that accelerate impact. The graphic above highlights the interventions that USAID's child health research agenda addresses in order to accelerate knowledge on how to deliver interventions equitably and efficiently while maintaining quality.

As part of research to observe and improve prescriber treatment practices, a study in Ghana tested an intervention that sent daily mobile phone text messages to encourage licensed chemical sellers to prescribe the recommended zinc and ORS for consumers. Results showed a discrepancy ficiently. Key findings from costing research in Malawi, Senegal and Rwanda helped in the developing, adapting and refining of an Excel-based model. The model will guide iCCM implementing countries to better plan and manage costs associated with introduction, scale-up and sustainment of their iCCM programs. USAID is also investing in a multicountry study in countries such as Malawi and Mali. This study is assessing the influences that hinder and support policies for iCCM introduction as well as tracking implementation progress. The key results will aid in developing policy recommendations for the introduction and scale-up of the iCCM programs and will help ministries of health, program managers and other stakeholders to better track the progress of iCCM programs.

Indoor air pollution

Indoor air pollution is responsible for the deaths of an estimated 1.6 million people annually. More than half of these deaths occur among children under 5 years of age. USAID encourages the use of fuel-efficient cook stoves rather than solid fuel because they effectively reduce indoor air pollution and lower the risks of acute lower respiratory infections in children. Indoor air pollution in developing countries is generated by inefficient stoves that burn wood, crop waste and dung and those that burn coal.

An Agency-funded survey in Kenya observed the indoor air pollution outcomes and the usage and perceptions of a new fuel-efficient cook stove technology introduced in households. The cook stoves marked significant progress in providing cleaner air quality within the home, showing decreases in the amounts of dangerous indoor air pollutants, i.e., decreases of 51 percent and 37 percent for particulate matter ($PM2.5$) and CO, respectively, while also gaining widespread approval from consumers.

Additional Agency-funded studies are testing the ways to expand fuel-efficient cook stoves by using behavior change communication. In Uganda, India and Bangladesh, research on consumer attitudes, social norms and lack of knowledge of fuel-efficient cook stoves is helping to inform the design of communication interventions, such as door-to-door visits by female community leaders, sale offers and demonstrations. The total research will advance USAID's commitment to the Global Alliance for Clean

Since 2008, USAID's Child Survival and Health Grants Program (CSHGP) has supported 19 international non-governmental organizations, in collaboration with academia, ministries of health and other local partners in 23 countries, to implement and test innovative approaches to end preventable child and maternal deaths through community-oriented interventions. Findings from some of the research projects are described below.

From 2008 to 2012, research funded by CSHGP in Nepal's Baitadi district tested an Enhanced Homestead Food Production model (EHFP) to reduce the rate of stunting, wasting, underweight and anemia. Through a collaboration between the Government of Nepal's agricultural and nutritional sectors, the EHFP model teaches households improved techniques for the year-round production of diversified animal and plant-source foods and uses interpersonal nutrition counseling and communication conveyed by health volunteers to promote optimal nutrition practices. Though the EHFP model successfully improved women's nutritional status, study results show that a longer time frame or a combination with other nutrition strategies may be needed to reverse child stunting in settings with extremely high prevalence of malnutrition such as in Baitadi. The findings are being used by USAID and the Government of Nepal to adapt and scale up this model in other areas of Nepal.

From 2009 to 2013, CSHGP funded an innovative Essential Obstetric and Newborn Care (EONC) model in collaboration with the Government of Ecuador. The EONC network model creates and uses a comprehensive provincial-level network that coordinates community- and facility-based services (public and private) and promotes coordinated service delivery along the continuum of care from the households to facilities. This network supports increased coverage and improved quality of care in vulnerable, indigenous communities, including in the health care centers and county hospitals in these regions. The EONC network established in Cotopaxi contributed to improvements in household maternal behaviors, such as an increase in exclusive breastfeeding, referral of home complications by a traditional birth attendant to facility (from 50 percent to 83 percent) and postpartum visits within 2 days of birth (from 4 percent to 70 percent), as well as significant trends in reducing neonatal mortality. The evidence influenced a decision by the Government of Ecuador for country-wide expansion, as part of a national initiative to reduce maternal and newborn mortality, including a dedicated budget and staffing in all provinces of Ecuador. The model will continue to be adapted in Ecuador appropriate to the setting and can be globally adapted across countries.

From 2008 to 2012, the Better Health for Afghan Mothers and Children project tested the use of mobile phone technology (mHealth) as a job aid for community health workers (CHWs) based on the American College of Nurse-Midwives' Home Based Life Saving Skills for maternal and newborn care. It is used as a communication tool to make faster emergency responses possible and to create a comprehensive network that links community members, a health facility and a maternity hospital. An evaluation of this project found an increase in pregnant women who received antenatal care; received skilled delivery at a health facility; coordinated with the facility for referral; had a birth plan that involved a health facility; and displayed increased knowledge of adverse pregnancy signs. Findings from this study indicate that using mobile technology supports CHWs in their daily activities of coordinating and providing care, and was easily used by non-literate female CHWs for promoting health knowledge in households. The findings are being communicated to local officials for consideration of uptake in remote areas, and mHealth is being adapted for use in Afghanistan and other countries.

Cookstoves, a public-private partnership launched in September 2010 to research the most effective ways to maximize fuel-efficient cook stove use, scale up its adoption to 100 million households by 2020 and minimize the threat of indoor air pollution on disease risks.

Water, sanitation and hygiene behaviors

Interventions that ensure safe drinking water, proper hand washing and correct and consistent use of basic sanitation can reduce diarrhea in children under 5 by 25 percent to 50 percent. Water-testing technology that detects bacteria in drinking water can prevent unnecessary occurrences of severe childhood diarrhea. Because it is high cost and requires specialized laboratory equipment for test results, water testing is oftentimes impractical for low-resource areas. In response to these challenges, USAID is investing in research and development of a new portable water-testing tool known as the Compartmentalized Bag Test (CBT).

CBT is a low-cost, electricity- and lab-free method for getting a microbial profile of drinking water. CBT relies on the use of three plastic compartments that can incubate cultures of bacteria, and it delivers accurate results on bacterial contamination within 18 to 48 hours. A completed study in Peru validated the new technol-ogy, showing no significant differences between water quality test results of the standard laboratory tests and the CBTs. Because testing water quality is one of the major barriers to sustaining safe drinking water programs, the progress made in this CBT field test will further USAID's goal to improve drinking water, especially in low-resource areas where children are the most vulnerable to illness.

Substantial population growth in urban areas and in urban slums is another cause of health concerns in children under age 5. USAID will be funding research to study water, sanitation and hygiene behaviors in high-population cities. By specifically comparing urban settings with low-population settings, the study will shed light on how diseases related to sanitation are transmitted. Findings will help develop evidence-based recommendations for future policies and for sanitation interventions that will aid in curbing childhood deaths related to water-borne diseases.

MEASUREMENT

In conjunction with A Promise Renewed, USAID, UNICEF and other stakeholders are exploring how new or enhanced data collection could contribute to improved mortality estimation in the dynamic study of child health, which is highly affected by other determinants, such as education, ac-cess and health policies. Effective planning of health interventions and program success in declining mortality rely on accurate mortality data. Vital registration systems are an essential source of information for monitoring mortality, but these systems are weak in the 24 USAID maternal and child health priority countries due to such factors as lack of capacity for postmortem examinations. USAID has successfully piloted sample vital registration with "verbal autopsy," which is a method that entails asking family members and health workers about the circumstances surrounding a death in order to determine the likely cause. This approach has been piloted in several settings, and now there are plans to scale it up.

USAID is also field testing an innovative system in Tanzania that is simpler than vital registration. This system uses an integrated data collection and statistical analysis platform for population and public health monitoring. It is a low-cost, sustainable and continuously operated monitoring system that combines the benefits of both sample surveys and surveillance systems for large populations over prolonged periods of time. Such approaches will allow us to produce more robust and timely child mortality estimates while concurrently addressing long-term issues of strengthening vital registration systems.

NUTRITION

BACKGROUND

More than 800 million people are chronically hungry, and millions suffer from micronutrient deficiencies. For example, almost half of pregnant women in the developing world are anemic, and iron-deficiency anemia is estimated to be a key factor in more than 25 percent of maternal deaths and in low birth weight infants. Chronic undernutrition in children, as measured by stunting in the first 2 years of life, affects 165 million children under 5 worldwide, which puts them at elevated risk of mortality and cognitive deficits and increased risk of adult obesity and noncommunicable diseases.

People suffer from chronic food insecurity not just because food supplies are inadequate, but also, and more importantly, because they cannot afford sufficient nutritious food or they are unable to access appropriate health care. When people are food insecure and undernourished, their economic potential is significantly impaired. The 2013 *Lancet* Series on maternal and child nutrition estimates that undernutrition inhibits a country's economy by at least 8 percent because of direct productivity losses, losses via poorer cognition and losses via reduced schooling. World Bank estimates of 2 percent to 3 percent of losses in global gross domestic product are from undernutrition and micronutrient deficiencies, amounting to $2 trillion annually. Undernutrition can cost individuals up to 10 percent of their lifetime earnings.

USAID research activities have been essential in establishing global evidence on effective approaches to reduce undernutrition. This information has been utilized to develop high-impact health and agriculture interventions to reduce undernutrition. Building on prior research findings, USAID aims to reduce undernutrition in 19 focus countries by 20 percent by 2016. In order to do so, USAID targets its nutrition programs on three main pathways: (1) the prevention of undernutrition during the critical 1,000-day window from pregnancy to 24 months; (2) the treatment of undernutrition in children under 5 through individual prevention programs, critical nutrition services (including the treatment of severe malnu-

trition) and the enhancement of nutrition competency; and (3) the promotion of an enabling policy environment. The nutrition strategy involves strategic collaboration with development partners working across sectors to scale up programs. Key to the nutrition research strategy is improving host country human and institutional capacity to conduct research and leverage the results to formulate policies and design programs.

RESEARCH AND INTRODUCTION AREAS

Integrated multisectoral approaches to improve nutrition outcomes, including stunting and maternal and child anemia

Long-term improvements in nutrition can only be achieved through multisectoral approaches that address food security, maternal and child feeding practices, access to clean water and sanitation and access to health services. Further evidence is needed on effective, affordable ways to communicate nutrition information to encourage families to make healthy decisions. A promising approach is through integration of nutrition education into existing agricultural sector programs that reach families and communities.

Building on a current agricultural extension program in India, a study is using hand-held video cameras to develop participatory, community-based educational videos with information that focuses specifically on nutrition needs during pregnancy and early childhood. If the videos prove to be an effective and feasible method for promoting nutrition and if they can be adapted to serve diverse populations, they can be candidates for wider distribution. The use of pico projectors means the videos can be downloaded from YouTube or other designated websites and subsequently shown without electricity or an Internet connection. Research on the effectiveness and feasibility of this innovation for the promotion of nutrition will help determine if the approach can be easily adapted and scaled to broaden diverse populations' access to nutrition information.

Additionally, USAID supported an approach to combine both nutrition and hygiene

into agriculture programs. This intervention built on an existing program in Bangladesh, where water and sanitation initiatives were integrated with nutrition projects. The results from the qualitative analysis helped develop the approach for future uses.

Agriculture and health programs can also coordinate through food fortification, which has been identified as one of the most cost-effective mechanisms to provide essential nutrients often missing in the diets of undernourished populations. USAID supports research on different fortification methodologies to be used by agriculture projects to improve the nutrient density of staple foods consumed by vulnerable rural populations. Initial findings demonstrated that modified processing procedures did little to enhance iron and zinc content, and adding fortificants to fertilizers used on staple crops more effectively increased nutrient density. Based on the findings of the feasibility and effectiveness of this fortification, this ongoing research will further demonstrate the nutrient availability and the market acceptability of fortified foods.

Implementation research for improved diet diversity and quality

Nutrient deficiencies, resulting in part from poor diet quality, impose significant risks of maternal and child morbidity and mortality. Recent peer-reviewed research has shown that women of reproductive age are often deficient in vitamin A, zinc, iodine, iron, folate and calcium. These deficiencies increase their risk of mortality at delivery, restrict fetal growth and lead to negative birth outcomes for infants. As a result of poor maternal nutrition, inadequate breastfeeding practices and insufficient complementary feeding, children under 5 continue to be significantly deficient in iron, zinc, iodine and vitamin A. These deficiencies, in turn, severely limit their growth and cognitive development.

In order to reduce the high prevalence of nutrient deficiencies among women and children, USAID is supporting multiyear, multicountry research in Asia and Africa that is examining the effect of enhancing diet quality through nutrient-dense food supplements to prevent and treat undernutrition. USAID is also evaluating new agriculture technologies and food processing adaptations to enhance the nutrient quality of different staple foods. USAID is continuing to support assessments of the coverage and quality of fortified foods at the regional and national levels in countries where women's and children's micronutrient deficiencies remain high.

Iron folate supplementation is important for pregnant women with anemia because it reduces the risk of maternal and infant complications, but supplies are often unavailable to women who need them. USAID is also developing an assessment tool using demographic and health data from multiple countries to evaluate distribution of micronutrient iron folate tablets for pregnant women through their respective health systems. Initial country analyses of results were completed in Malawi, Ethiopia, Rwanda and Nigeria. Results from all four countries pointed to patterns in delivery failure of micronutrient supplementation and identified opportunities for improvement. Additional countries will be added to the analysis to support an outline of specific recommendations for a quality micronutrient supplement distribution system for maternal anemia programs.

Measurement tools for nutrition programs and policies
Many countries with high rates of undernutrition lack access to appropriate, cost-effective technologies and tools to help identify and combat undernutrition. Currently, USAID is testing the effectiveness of new technologies to identify nutritional

deficiencies. Such technologies are critical to increasing the effectiveness and coverage of nutrition programs. Standardized indicators developed through USAID's support are guiding policy improvements.

Despite the significant negative ramifications of anemia, interventions that identify the disorder and provide the best treatment are difficult to scale up due to cost, availability of testing equipment, stock outs and the failure of the supply chain to reach those most in need. Existing invasive testing, such as blood testing, is costly and requires regular delivery of supplies, limiting the identification of mothers at risk of anemia. USAID continues to confront these barriers by supporting research on the effectiveness of a noninvasive anemia screening device for pregnant women. This device requires no additional supplies and can be used outside of health clinics, enabling increased coverage of testing. Pending results from the study, USAID plans to conduct additional activities to generate demand for the device and create sustainable costing models for large-scale uptake in targeted countries.

USAID supports the development of nutrition indicators that effectively measure hunger levels and dietary quality and diversity. These internationally validated measurement tools assess the baseline conditions in countries and the effects of nutrition programs on health. For example, in countries such as Kenya, Bangladesh and Mozambique, one set of tools evaluated the nutrition sensitivity of agriculture value chains. The tools assisted each country to

design programs and recognize new ways to improve nutrition outcomes.

Other tools developed with USAID support helped identify specific nutrient gaps in women's and children's diets and in child feeding practices. This information was then used to inform program design to better target social and behavior change communication.

A modeling tool to substantiate the correlation between low birth weight and the development of noncommunicable diseases in later life will be validated in the coming year using multiple country data sets. The Agency also continues to support the use of advocacy tools to aid governments in revising policies, so they address their context-specific nutrition problems.

With over 50 million children suffering from acute undernutrition, also known as wasting, treatment continues to be a priority research area for USAID. To improve treatment of wasting and increase its coverage, the Agency supported research to implement and scale up community-based management of acute malnutrition (CMAM) programs. CMAM is an approach to detect early cases of child malnutrition and treat children with ready-to-use nutritional foods and nutrient-dense foods. The program has been rolled out in countries across Asia and Africa. To continue CMAM progress, USAID is analyzing tools that allow community workers to more simply identify wasted children, monitor their progress and discharge patients from the program when they have reached their target weight.

PROMOTING INNOVATION AND SCALING FOR IMPACT

Multiple lifesaving health technologies have been developed to address some of the world's most pressing global health challenges, yet many of these promising technologies fail to reach all who need them. A recent review of a World Health Organization database revealed that only 4 percent of low-income countries had begun utilizing key global health technologies within 10 years of regulatory approval. To speed up access to, and utilization of, lifesaving interventions, USAID established the Center for Accelerating Innovation and Impact to promote innovative, business-minded solutions to these enduring problems. The Center supports USAID's overarching global health objectives by:

Identifying Market Tools for Innovation and Acceleration: USAID draws on state-of-the-art practices to develop a range of impact-accelerating tools to be leveraged throughout the broader global health community.

- *Product Launch and Scale-Up Tools* – By developing product introduction and uptake planning tools that adapt industry best practices, we are cutting the time it takes to transform "discoveries in the lab" to "impact on the ground."

- *Market Shaping Toolkit* – As a field of research, market shaping explores the application of market-based approaches to address market failures and deficiencies. By advancing our knowledge and application of this research, we are better able to support well-functioning health care markets capable of delivering lower prices and higher quality for end-users while preserving incentives for companies to invest in innovation. Given the promise of this relatively new field, a toolkit is under development to inform and guide market-shaping activities to address market shortcomings and achieve better value for money.

- *Innovation Labs* – Convene periodic meetings between luminaries and technical experts in innovation, product introduction and utilization across multiple sectors to share learning and best practices. Since launching in June of 2013, three Innovation Labs – two on Product Introduction and one on Market Dynamics – were held at USAID training facilities.

Driving Innovation and Partnerships: USAID is harnessing the power of innovators to find better ways to do business. To help drive innovation and partnerships, the Center is working closely with the private sector, universities, non-governmental organizations and other key stakeholders to leverage core competencies and fill evidence gaps around priority health technologies and interventions.

- *Saving Lives at Birth: A Grand Challenge for Development* – Since 2011, USAID has invested in 61 potentially groundbreaking innovations to dramatically reduce maternal and newborn deaths and stillbirths in parts of the world that suffer from limited access to electricity, poor road conditions and lack of transportation, low literacy levels and too few health care workers. Saving Lives at Birth – a $50 million partnership between USAID, the Government of Norway, the Bill & Melinda Gates Foundation, Grand Challenges Canada and the United Kingdom Department for International Development – is a global call for transformational ideas, with the potential for substantial and sustainable impact over time. The first two rounds of the challenge were highly successful, attracting more than 1,100 applications from across the world. These rounds supported production of innovations, such as an inhaled form of oxytocin to prevent postpartum hemorrhage; a "solar suitcase" to provide light and electricity to medical providers; and the national scale-up of chlorhexidine cord care in Nepal to prevent newborn deaths due to infection. Round III awards were announced in the summer of 2013.

- *Xcellerator* – In partnership with the Lemelson Foundation and the National Collegiate Inventors and Innovators Alliance, this program provides global health innovators with training and mentorship to ensure well-designed pathways to scale.

- *Social Entrepreneurship Accelerator at Duke (SEAD)* – As part of the Higher Education Solutions Network, Duke University uses an ecosystem approach to scale the impact of global health social enterprises that have already shown promising results. SEAD will evaluate and share knowledge regarding common barriers to scale and scaling strategies.

- *PEER Health* – This supports partnerships between researchers at universities in developing countries and the National Institutes of Health to advance critical evidence, build research capacity and strengthen collaboration between local public health institutions, practitioners and country governments. In the first cycle, 16 individual awards were made to researchers in 10 countries.

Accelerating Introduction and Scale-Up: Utilizing market-based solutions and industry best practices can increase access to lifesaving technologies for underserved populations. USAID is supporting the rapid adoption of products and interventions in target regions and is developing innovative financing mechanisms to accelerate product development and access for high-priority health innovations.

- Introduction and Scale-Up of Priority Health Commodities:
  - Amoxicillin – Through demand forecasting and engagement with suppliers, in partnership with UNICEF's Supply Division, USAID is catalyzing the development of business plans for these potential manufacturers and exploring possible market-shaping interventions, such as addressing country-level bottlenecks in manufacturing, procurement and distribution.
  - Chlorhexidine – USAID is supporting the design and execution of market research and demand forecasting in Nigeria in the development of a national introduction strategy.
  - Injectable antibiotics – USAID is contributing to the development of a manufacturer landscape analysis to understand opportunities and constraints in supplying injectable antibiotics.
  - ORS and Zinc – Working with members of the U.N. Pneumonia and Diarrhea Working Group, USAID is partnering with McCann Healthcare, a global health care communications firm, to strengthen demand for zinc and ORS in 10 high-burden countries.

FAMILY PLANNING AND REPRODUCTIVE HEALTH

BACKGROUND

It is estimated that 222 million women in developing countries want to space or limit child bearing but are not using a modern method of family planning. Factors that contribute to this unmet need include inadequate or inaccurate information among couples, poor access to reproductive health services and contraceptive methods that are seen as inconvenient or too expensive.

Voluntary family planning, respectful of the rights of individuals and couples to choose freely the timing, spacing and number of children they want, contributes to the health and well-being of women and their children. Health benefits result directly from fewer unintended pregnancies, fewer abortions and longer birth intervals. If all women in developing countries who want to avoid pregnancy used an effective contraceptive method, the number of maternal deaths would fall an additional 30 percent from current levels. If all births were spaced at least 2 years apart, the risk of death would be reduced by 10 percent in infancy and by 21 percent among children ages 1 to 4 years. In addition to these health-related benefits, a woman's ability to choose the number, timing and spacing of her children can have consequences for her educational attainment, labor force participation and earnings, which, in turn, affect the well-being of her children, household and community.

USAID advances and supports voluntary family planning programs that enable countries to respond to the needs of their people. Research for family planning and reproductive health supports the development of novel technologies and methods. Implementation research helps to improve the efficiency of family planning programming approaches, reduce barriers to services, promote method acceptability and continuation and find new ways to expand services, so they reach underserved women and their families. Among women with an unmet need for family planning, many barriers underlie nonuse of contraception, incorrect use and discontinuation – all of which can result in an unintended pregnancy. These barriers can include concerns about side effects, misperceptions about the risk of pregnancy, opposition from partners or others and inadequate knowledge about contraception and fertile periods. Challenges getting supplies due to limited clinic hours and provider preparation and to long distances to service delivery points compound the problem. In addition, women may find contraceptive methods inconvenient to use, expensive or inappropriate for their needs. Certain groups, especially young, never-married women, postpartum women and women living in rural and underserved peri-urban areas, have a much higher level of unmet need for family planning.

RESEARCH AND INTRODUCTION AREAS

Improving contraceptive methods

To combat the barriers to contraception use among women with an unmet need for family planning, biomedical research seeks to (1) refine existing contraceptive methods to make them more acceptable, affordable and accessible and (2) develop new contraceptive methods that better meet the family planning needs of women and their families.

USAID supported the completion of studies required for U.S. Food and Drug Administration approval of the 1-year contraceptive vaginal ring – the first woman-controlled, long-acting family planning method. Manufacturing refinements were also completed to reduce the ring's overall cost. Additionally, early phases of development began for two new combination vaginal rings, tenofovir/levonogestrel and dapivirine/levonogestrel, which are designed to prevent unintended pregnancy and protect against HIV and other sexually transmitted infections.

USAID is partnering with the United Kingdom Department for International Development, the Bill & Melinda Gates Foundation and others to support the pilot introduction of a contraceptive packaged in a pre-filled, single-use, subcutaneous injection device called Sayana Press™. This unique system is easier to use and more portable than many other options, allowing trained community providers to use Sayana Press™ right in the home. Acceptability studies in Uganda and Senegal showed that clients preferred receiving injectable contraception with Sayana Press™ compared with a standard syringe and needle, citing fewer side effects, faster administration and less pain. In Uganda, 84 percent of study participants said they would select Sayana Press™ over the standard intramuscular injection if both were available, and all 34

EXPANDING CONTRACEPTIVE OPTIONS THROUGH THE SILCS DIAPHRAGM

The SILCS diaphragm is a "one-size-fits-most" reusable, nonhormonal contraceptive barrier method that does not require a pelvic exam. The diaphragm recently received regulatory approval to be sold on the European market, which is an important step in expanding nonhormonal contraceptive options for women in developing countries. USAID has been involved in this important multiyear, multipartner collaborative effort since its inception. Previous USAID support allowed for large-scale contraceptive effectiveness and safety studies of the SILCS diaphragm. USAID-supported studies in the Dominican Republic, South Africa, Thailand and the United States have validated the acceptability of the SILCS diaphragm among women and their partners. To expand women-controlled options to manage their fertility and protect against HIV and sexually transmitted infections, the SILCS diaphragm can address several of the most common reasons for unmet need, including concerns about side effects and the desire for a method that can be used at the time of sex. Additionally, when paired with gels that protect against HIV and sexually transmitted infections, the SILCS diaphragm has the potential to serve as the first true multipurpose prevention technology.

providers interviewed preferred giving injectable contraceptive with Sayana Press™ over the standard intramuscular injection with syringe and needle. Similar results were found in a second study in Senegal. Providers preferred the new method largely because the prefilled, all-in-one design made preparation and administration easier and faster. Clients' main reasons for selecting it included experiencing fewer side effects, fast administration, less pain and method effectiveness.

Access to family planning and reproductive health services

USAID implementation research is helping to improve the efficiency and effectiveness of programs in developing countries. It informs the design of culturally appropriate programs and service delivery approaches in order to address gaps, develop tools and materials to improve provider performance, test solutions to overcome barriers to services and expand successful evidence-based practices to underserved women and their families.

Community health workers (CHWs) have made family planning and reproductive health methods and services more accessible. For example, in Ethiopia, CHWs now have the skills to safely insert contraceptive implants. In Nigeria and Kenya, USAID-supported research led to changes in health policy to allow CHWs to provide popular injectable contraception. In Guatemala and the Democratic Republic of the Congo, USAID research in populations with low literacy rates showed that CHWs with little health background can successfully integrate fertility awareness methods into their outreach activities. Engaging CHWs in efforts to address unmet need is particularly important for helping hard-to-reach populations.

Unmet need for family planning, defined as the percentage of women who do not want to become pregnant who are not using contraception, is found worldwide but is highest in African countries (see graphic). To enlist technology in addressing the unmet needs for family planning and reproductive health, USAID has contributed to a growing body of research on the feasibility and effectiveness of using mobile phones. Mobile phone use has expanded rapidly in developing countries in recent years, presenting new opportunities for sharing information and referrals for family planning and reproductive health services.

This approach has been particularly effective for reaching youth and men. Through public-private partnerships with mobile phone companies, USAID has helped make accurate family planning and reproductive health information more widely available and accessible. In India, a phone-based application (or app) for the Standard Days Method has been developed and tested and is now being scaled up.

USAID-supported research also tested a variety of innovative models to address social, cultural and other factors affecting the use of family planning and reproductive health services. Research studies that focus on an individual country include an emphasis on scalable tools and interventions, as well as cost analyses, so lessons learned can be applied in other settings.

One study in India is evaluating a government-run program to prevent child marriage through conditional cash transfer, in other words, providing money to families under the condition they do not marry off their daughters as children. The evaluation of the India conditional cash transfer program is currently under way. The evaluation will assess whether the program helped delay early marriage, which is linked to subsequent early childbearing/high-risk pregnancies. Formative research on the study population has documented parents' and guardians' awareness of the negative effects of early childbearing on health outcomes. Impact results are expected in the next year.

Another study in northern Uganda developed culturally appropriate interventions to promote positive attitudes and behaviors about reproductive health among adolescents. The Gender Roles, Equality and Transformation (GREAT) model includes a radio drama to catalyze discussion and change; a toolkit to promote reflection and dialogue; a community action cycle to mobilize key community leaders to strengthen their capacity to promote and sustain change; community-level activities that recognize and celebrate people who demonstrate a commitment to gender-equitable behaviors; and training for Village Health Teams to improve access and quality of youth-friendly sexual and reproductive health services. The interventions are currently being implemented and evaluated.

Healthy timing and spacing of pregnancies

Studies have found an association between births that are spaced at least 2 years apart and significantly lower rates of mortality, morbidity, underweight and stunting of children under 5 years of age. To develop better family planning counseling tools and interventions for the future, USAID supported a rigorous review to produce a more precise understanding of how differences in the amount of time between births can contribute to differences in health outcomes for children. Researchers found new evidence suggesting that short birth intervals may be linked with higher risk of infection from mother to child through the placenta or during delivery; postpartum weakness of the cervix, which

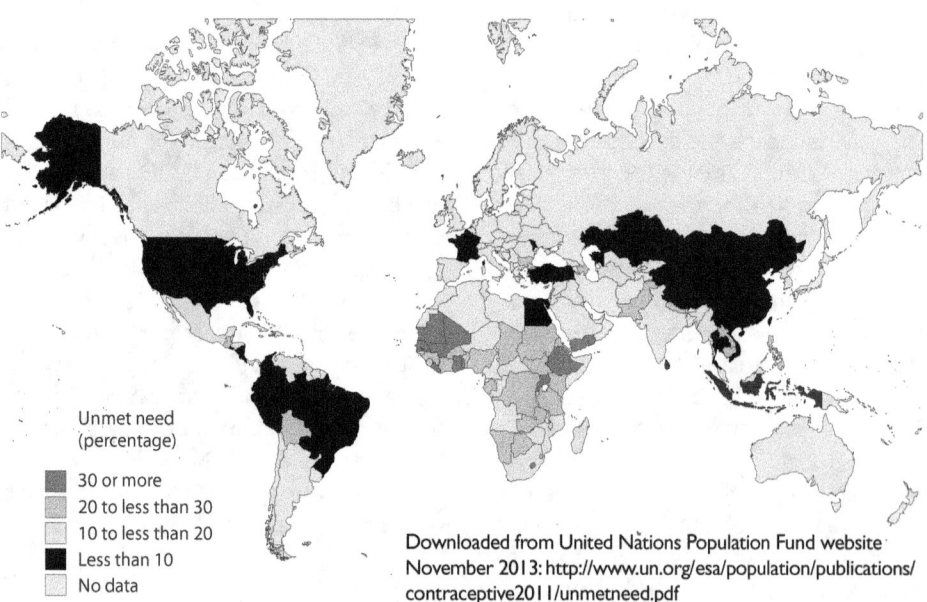

Unmet Need for Family Planning, 2011

Unmet need (percentage)

- 30 or more
- 20 to less than 30
- 10 to less than 20
- Less than 10
- No data

may lead to preterm birth in the next pregnancy; postpartum folate (vitamin B9) depletion that causes poor perinatal outcomes; and changes in the immune properties of breastmilk when an elder sibling is also being breastfed.

Another study that looked at the relationship between family planning and child survival in Bangladesh generated new evidence on interventions to support healthy timing of births. The intervention that was studied involved educating families on using the Lactational Amenorrhea Method (LAM). This scientific approach allows women to safely rely on breastfeeding as a family planning method and to practice exclusive breastfeeding for a longer period of time. Groups using LAM showed significantly higher rates of modern method use than controls – 36 percent versus 16 percent – during the 6 months following birth. Also, they were more likely to continue family planning methods and less likely to be pregnant 30 months after delivery. Women in the intervention areas experienced longer duration of exclusive breastfeeding, higher family planning continuation rates at 30 months postpartum and lower likelihood of becoming pregnant by 30 months postpartum.

HIV AND AIDS

BACKGROUND

Great strides have been made in combating the HIV and AIDS pandemic. With 20 percent less infections now than 10 years ago, HIV and AIDS are sharply declining in some regions. However, an estimated 2.5 million people continue to be newly infected with HIV every year. In sub-Saharan Africa, 1 in 20 adults are living with HIV, and in the Middle East and North Africa, new infections have increased by over 35 percent in the last decade. Women and girls account for more than half of the 34 million people living with HIV worldwide and for 58 percent of the cases in sub-Saharan Africa.

While no single approach to HIV and AIDS prevention is likely to have a sufficient impact, integrated behavioral, biomedical and structural interventions yield the best results. Though HIV prevention methods are available, the need to develop and evaluate novel technologies and evidence-based strategies is as urgent as ever if the course of the pandemic is to be reversed and an AIDS-free generation achieved.

USAID's research agenda contributes to the HIV and AIDS response and continues to harness USAID's extensive health and development expertise to maximize the reach of technically sound, cost-effective and sustainable HIV and AIDS interventions. Through 2013, USAID continued to collaborate with key partners dedicated to the development of an HIV vaccine and effective microbicides while furthering the existing evidence base to improve HIV and AIDS programming. USAID supports the development of safe, effective, acceptable and affordable microbicide candidates, including two advanced leads in Phase III trials. USAID also funds novel microbicide delivery approaches and multipurpose microbicides in the hopes of bringing diverse options to market for women. The development and testing of novel HIV vaccine candidates for global use remain a high priority. HIV vaccine research and testing are supported by long-term epidemiological studies and research into access and policy issues, and they are strengthening clinical trial and laboratory capacity in developing countries. Through implementa-

tion science research, USAID is improving access to quality and effective HIV and AIDS prevention, treatment, care and support and service delivery programs in the prevention of mother-to-child transmission of HIV (PMTCT) in developing countries. Implementation research and program evaluations identify and address gaps in knowledge and increase the evidence base for scaling up promising approaches for improving programs.

RESEARCH AND INTRODUCTION AREAS

Microbicides for women to reduce the risk of HIV infection

In many countries, women lack the power to negotiate the use of existing prevention tools and approaches to protect themselves against HIV. At the same time, women make up 60 percent of new infections in sub-Saharan Africa. There is a need for HIV prevention methods that women can control on their own.

In 2010, a USAID-funded trial conducted by the Centre for the AIDS Programme of Research in South Africa (CAPRISA 004) provided groundbreaking proof of concept that 1-percent tenofovir gel can safely and effectively reduce a woman's risk of HIV infection. A confirmatory trial, the Follow-on African Consortium for Tenofovir Studies (FACTS) 001 trial, using the same application regimen as in CAPRISA 004, aims to achieve regulatory approval for this product. Now in its second year, FACTS 001 is enrolling participants at nine trial sites in South Africa. This trial is supported by USAID in partnership with the South African Department of Science and Technology and the Bill & Melinda Gates Foundation.

With the unprecedented opportunity in the next 5 years to obtain regulatory approval from the U.S. Food and Drug Administration for 1-percent tenofovir gel, there is an urgent need to plan for the introduction of this new prevention product in countries where it will have the greatest impact. With USAID collaboration, the new public-private joint venture, Propreven, is preparing to register, manufacture and distribute 1-percent tenofovir gel in various African countries.

USAID and its partners are implementing the Agency's Proposal for a Shared Vision and Strategic Plan for Microbicide Introduction to prepare for the introduction and access programs that will be needed. The Agency is also initiating implementation studies and planning for operations research. This includes the CAPRISA 008 study, supported jointly by USAID and South Africa, to compare the use of 1-percent tenofovir gel when provided in a clinical trial setting with its use when provided in a more typical family planning program setting.

Enhanced formulations, dosing regimens and delivery methods for both coitally associated and coitally independent methods are also being developed and tested. Year 2 of The Ring Study, a Phase III clinical trial of the dapivirine vaginal ring, is under way with support from USAID and other donors. This trial is the first time a nongel microbicide delivery system is being tested for effectiveness in women. Other microbicide formulations are beginning clinical testing and may prove to be more acceptable to users. If they are, these formulations may also be more effectively used. They include a 90-day tenofovir vaginal ring and fast-dissolving vaginal tablets. These options may be easier for some women to use and may reduce the cost of microbicides further.

Microbicide candidates that have multipurpose prevention activity are also in development and may be very attractive to potential users and providers. In addition to providing protection against HIV infection, these microbicide candidates may, for example, protect against other sexually transmitted infections and unwanted pregnancies. Early testing has begun on vaginal rings that produce combined contraceptive and anti-HIV activity.

To better predict when a new microbicide candidate warrants the investment required for advanced product development and testing in Phase III clinical trials, USAID continues to collaborate with its partners and other donors to design and validate improved models for preclinical evaluation and for Phase I, II and III clinical trials. These results help USAID ensure that its resourc-

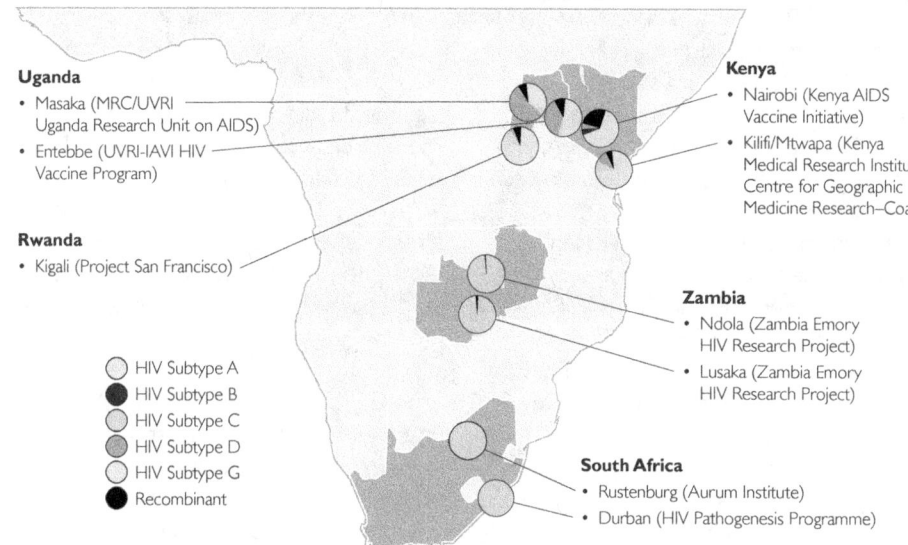

RESEARCH CAPACITY ESTABLISHED IN AFRICA BY IAVI AND ITS PARTNERS

Uganda
- Masaka (MRC/UVRI Uganda Research Unit on AIDS)
- Entebbe (UVRI-IAVI HIV Vaccine Program)

Rwanda
- Kigali (Project San Francisco)

- ○ HIV Subtype A
- ● HIV Subtype B
- ○ HIV Subtype C
- ○ HIV Subtype D
- ○ HIV Subtype G
- ● Recombinant

Kenya
- Nairobi (Kenya AIDS Vaccine Initiative)
- Kilifi/Mtwapa (Kenya Medical Research Institute; Centre for Geographic Medicine Research–Coast)

Zambia
- Ndola (Zambia Emory HIV Research Project)
- Lusaka (Zambia Emory HIV Research Project)

South Africa
- Rustenburg (Aurum Institute)
- Durban (HIV Pathogenesis Programme)

IAVI clinical research centers coordinate with and refer to PEPFAR treatment centers.

es are used as effectively as possible.

HIV vaccine candidates

USAID supports the International AIDS Vaccine Initiative (IAVI) to strengthen clinical trial capacity in developing countries, enrich the pipeline and advance the development and testing of novel HIV vaccine candidates and analyze policy and future access issues through a cooperative agreement (see graphic above). In 2012, IAVI and its partners tested three HIV vaccine candidates in Africa through Phase I trials at IAVI-supported clinical research centers. These trials have enrolled efficiently, are gender balanced and have particularly high volunteer retention. A novel approach to vaccine delivery, known as electroporation, which uses tiny electrical pulses to increase the immune responses elicited by DNA vaccines by increasing the cellular uptake of an agent by 1,000 times or more, was employed and was well received by East African volunteers. Lastly, one of IAVI's principal vaccine design platforms, Adeno 35, a low sero-prevalent human adenovirus vector, was shown to be safe, well tolerated and capable of stimulating robust immune responses. These trials have led to IAVI to use a new vector, SeV-G, derived from a weak-ened form of the Sendai virus, a virus related to the measles and canine distemper viruses. The vector was developed by IAVI and the Japanese biotechnology company DNAVEC as a novel, replicating viral vector that targets mucosal tissues and carries the gene for the gag protein of HIV as a vaccine antigen. The trial will assess immune responses elicited by a prime-boost regimen of SeV-G and a vac-

cine candidate based on adenovirus serotype 35.

IAVI epidemiological studies contribute to rational vaccine trial design and public health planning to shape HIV prevention in communities and countries where IAVI works. Four long-term epidemiological studies conducted by IAVI and its clinical partners in Africa continue to inform HIV vaccine design and testing. They included HIV incidence studies in key populations, such as men who have sex with men on the Kenyan coast and underserved men and women in fishing communities around Lake Victoria. IAVI actively follows these studies' key cohorts of volunteers to track their acute and early HIV infection and refers them to treatment programs as needed. This past year, IAVI and partners identified important differences in the progression of HIV infection to AIDS, the time to antiretroviral therapy initiation and differences in CD4 T cell values among African and European populations that may inform HIV care and treatment.

IAVI continues to work closely with the Joint United Nations Programme on HIV/AIDS and the AIDS Vaccine Advocacy Co-alition to review Good Participatory Practice (GPP) guidelines, which are designed to engage communities and stakeholders in biomedical HIV prevention research. GPP evaluation tools were piloted at eight African clinical research centers. As part of the GPP, in 2012, IAVI's clinical partners in Africa provided free HIV voluntary coun-

seling and testing (VCT) to over 47,000 individuals. Since 2004, more than 300,000 individuals have received HIV VCT through IAVI-supported research.

With collaborators, IAVI accelerated its broadly neutralizing antibody program on an aggressive timeline in order to translate the best ideas into clinical candidates. By the end of 2012, IAVI had selected the first three antigen candidates for early product development. All three are designed to elicit broadly neutralizing antibodies for fighting HIV. This is a significant milestone in the HIV vaccine research field, which is now using the knowledge drawn from the study of these powerful HIV-blocking proteins to design new vaccine concepts.

Implementation science for prevention, care and treatment programs

The first phase of the U.S. President's Emergency Plan for AIDS Relief (PEPFAR) focused on reducing HIV mortality and morbidity as quickly as possible. The main priority of the emergency response in the first phase was rapid scale-up of HIV and AIDS service delivery programs. Building off the first phase, the second phase of PEPFAR focuses on increasing the sustainability, cost-effectiveness and impact of HIV and AIDS programs. Adopting approaches that increase the impact of programs and make them more sustainable and cost-effective will ensure the continuation of long-standing, locally owned HIV programs in the countries that are hardest hit by the epidemic. In order to achieve these outcomes, PEPFAR embraces an "implementation science" framework to improve the uptake, translation and implementation of research into service delivery practices. USAID's implementation science agenda emphasizes methodological rigor, programmatic context and sound scientific principles in support of HIV and AIDS prevention, care and treatment research. Ongoing implementation science research and program evaluations aim to provide local implementing partners, donors and national governments with the evidence base to improve HIV and AIDS services and to inform policy.

In 2012 and 2013, USAID awarded more than $26 million to support 11 implementation science studies in 10 countries. The purpose of these studies was to answer critical questions across a range of health program areas and populations to strengthen the integration of programs across the HIV prevention, care and treatment continuum. The studies' findings will contribute to the evidence base for HIV programs and will maximize the impact of program investments around the world. Data gathered will help partner countries to support their efforts to prevent new infections and save lives. Additional studies are anticipated to emphasize program-specific and cross-cutting issues that the current studies are not addressing.

USAID is supporting research and evaluations to improve the coverage, quality and effectiveness of HIV and AIDS treatment and prevention programs. Projects receiving such USAID support include:

• The Research to Prevention (R2P) Project supports research to identify the most effective interventions for preventing HIV and improving HIV prevention programs in the countries most affected by the HIV epidemic. R2P seeks to achieve this goal by conducting applied research and program evaluation, pro-moting the utilization of data in program design and building local research capacity. R2P will end in March 2014 with more than 30 studies and activities completed. Results from a multicountry study called the *Systematic Monitoring of Voluntary Medical Male Circumcision Scale-up in Eastern and Southern Africa* showed that safe, high-quality voluntary medical male circumcision can be implemented and sustained at scale via a number of efficiency elements. Results from formative work undertaken in Swaziland on key populations revealed high levels of HIV and sexually transmitted infection prevalence among female sex workers and men who have sex with men; identified biological, behavioral and structural risk factors; and described the social context of these populations, including multilayered experiences of stigma.

• The HIVCore Project supports research that seeks to improve the efficiency, effectiveness, scale and quality of HIV and AIDS treatment, care and support and PMTCT programs by conducting operations research and focused evaluations and by promoting the use of research findings. HIVCore will end in September 2016 and anticipates having more than 20 different studies completed by then. To date, results from a multicountry assessment include findings that increase our understanding of how to make HIV programming more inclusive for persons with disabilities as they experience greater sexual vulnerability to HIV, lack access to HIV prevention and services and experience stigma that affects utilization of HIV services.

• The Gender-Based Violence (GBV) Program Evaluation identifies and addresses gaps in GBV prevention and service delivery through intensive monitoring and evaluation of GBV programs. It provides tools and methods to evaluate promising service delivery and community-based intervention models for GBV prevention and related HIV outcomes. The activity strengthens collaboration with local partners to bolster the evidence base for improving and scaling up effective GBV programs worldwide.

MALARIA

BACKGROUND

Malaria is a mosquito-borne disease caused by a parasite. People with malaria often experience fever, chills and flu-like illness. Left untreated, they may develop severe complications and die. According to the World Health Organization (WHO), the estimated number of global malaria deaths has fallen by more than one-third – from about 985,000 in 2000 to about 660,000 in 2010. In spite of this progress, malaria remains one of the major public health problems in Africa, with about 80 percent of malaria deaths occurring in African children under 5 years of age.

Children under 5 and pregnant women are especially at risk. In many African countries, 30 percent or more of outpatient visits and hospital admissions of children under 5 are reported to be caused by malaria. Malaria continues to place a heavy burden on individual families and national health systems. Because most malaria transmission occurs in rural areas, the greatest burden of the disease usually falls on families with lower incomes and whose access to health care is most limited.

Current control measures are highly effective and include long-lasting insecticide-treated nets (ITNs), indoor residual spraying (IRS), intermittent preventive treatment for pregnant women (IPTp) and prompt diagnosis and treatment with artemisinin-based combination therapy (ACT).

At the same time, challenges such as insecticide and drug resistance have emerged. New tools such as vaccines, new drugs and innovative mosquito control methods are needed to further support malaria prevention and control efforts, but these are at least several years away. USAID is committed to supporting research on these new tools and to answering key operational research questions in partnership with research partners around the globe and other U.S. Government departments and agencies, such as the Centers for Disease Control and Prevention (CDC), the National Institutes of Health (NIH) and the Department of Defense (DOD).

RESEARCH AND INTRODUCTION AREAS

Safe and effective vaccines for malaria
The vision of the USAID Malaria Vaccine Development Program (MVDP) is to end malaria as a major global health problem. The current set of malaria prevention and treatment tools are effective and have resulted in unprecedented reductions in malaria morbidity and mortality in many African countries. However, as long as conditions remain favorable for its transmission, malaria can only be truly controlled once a highly effective vaccine against clinical malaria becomes available. This is the long-term goal of the MVDP. Currently, a malaria vaccine developed by GlaxoSmithKline (GSK) is completing Phase III field evaluation and may become available within a few years, but it has a relatively low efficacy of 30 percent to 50 percent, and protection appears to be short lived. A more efficacious and durable vaccine is clearly needed.

There is little doubt that the development of a vaccine with the required attributes is possible, but this will very likely take many years to achieve. In the near term, the MVDP aims to demonstrate the feasibility of developing one or more highly efficacious vaccines (proof of concept) in order to inform decisions about investments in an actual product. It will inform these decisions in three ways: (1) by performing research to better understand the impediments to vaccine performance; (2) by producing investigational vaccines based on the most promising concepts; and (3) by evaluating these investigational vaccines for safety and efficacy in preclinical and clinical trials and field investigation.

Effective and affordable malaria medicines
Antimalarial drug resistance remains a global concern. One important way to defend against drug resistance is by developing new medicines to treat and prevent malaria that are effective and affordable. Though resistance to artemisinin drugs has not yet been documented in sub-Saharan Africa, if this were to emerge and spread, it would represent a major setback for malaria control efforts on the continent.

Since 2004, USAID has supported the Medicines for Malaria Venture (MMV), a public-private partnership, to catalyze antimalarial drug development. The MMV's emphasis is to develop drugs that are effective against resistant strains of *Plasmodium falciparum* and are safe for young children and pregnant women – the groups most vulnerable to malaria. Currently, the venture is partnering with more than 50 biotechnology and pharmaceutical companies. Through these partnerships, the venture is able to access a diverse array of novel and proprietary compound libraries. The information gained from these resources is informing efforts to boost the diversity of candidate drugs. USAID support has contributed to the MMV's noteworthy achievements, which include:

USAID Malaria Research

Optimize Existing Interventions
- Mosquito net durability
- Insecticide resistance
- Use of diagnostics for accurate malaria treatment
- Effectiveness of malaria prevention and treatment during pregnancy

Develop New Tools
- Malaria vaccines
  - Barriers to vaccine development
  - Investigational vaccine production and evaluation
- Malaria medicines
  - Develop drugs that are effective against resistant parasites and are safe in pregnant women and children

- More than 50 unique compounds are in various stages of the research and development pipeline.

- A new ACT, pyronaridine-artesunate, has received strict regulatory authority approval from the European Medicines Authority.

- Injectable artesunate, an alternative to quinine, has received WHO prequalification and is now being recommended by WHO as the preferred treatment for severe malaria. More than 3.2 million treatments have already been delivered to countries, and many other countries are adopting this as their first-line treatment for severe malaria.

- Clinical trials are under way for new candidate compounds from three unique classes of antimalarial drugs, including synthetic peroxides, spiroindolones and imidazolopiperazines. These new treatments offer the potential to address the emerging problem of ACT resistance that has developed in the Greater Mekong subregion.

*Malaria control program
implementation and impact*
Through the President's Malaria Initiative (PMI), which is led by USAID and implemented with CDC, USAID is conducting operational research focused on the practical challenges and bottlenecks related to the scale-up and sustainability of malaria prevention and treatment measures. This research focuses on program-relevant questions and is intended to complement the more upstream vaccine and drug development work funded by USAID and other U.S. Government departments and agencies, such as DOD and NIH.

PMI supports operational research studies on topics such as mosquito net durability and the effectiveness of combining interventions, such as IRS and ITNs. Looking forward, PMI will research the effect of insecticide resistance on ITN effectiveness, better use of diagnostics for accurate malaria treatment and the effectiveness of preventive malaria treatment during pregnancy in an environment of increasing resistance. PMI uses study results to help guide its program investments, make policy recommendations to national malaria control programs and target interventions to increase their cost-effectiveness. As the burden of malaria falls in sub-Saharan Africa, operational research will help programs adjust to the changing epidemiological landscape. The following are examples of PMI-funded operational research studies and their findings:

Nine PMI focus countries (Angola, Benin, Kenya, Malawi, Mozambique, Nigeria, Rwanda, Senegal and Zambia) are conducting studies on the physical and insecticidal longevity of ITNs. Overall study results have shown that many mosquito nets do not last the expected 3 years due to loss of physical integrity. Thus, ITNs may need to be replaced more frequently than previously anticipated in order to maintain high coverage. These findings are being used to inform research on ITN care-and-repair behaviors as well as to aid in design changes to ITNs to improve their physical durability.

Since 2008, the prevalence of malaria parasites in Zanzibar has been less than 1 percent. A study to evaluate the need to continue the country's IPTp program found that, of 1,321 women giving birth who did not receive the preventive treatment during pregnancy, only 4 had evidence of placental malaria. These results will help the Tanzania Ministry of Health decide whether to continue its program or implement alternative methods to protect pregnant women from adverse outcomes of malaria infection.

In Kenya, where mosquitoes have developed resistance to pyrethroid insecticides used in IRS campaigns, PMI supported a study to assess the effect of nine different insecticides or insecticide formulations on mosquito populations. Results were presented to the national vector control technical working group, which then made recommendations to the National Malaria Control Program to use a carbamate insecticide in future IRS campaigns due to its effectiveness and longevity in the study.

In Uganda, a study on the effectiveness of door-to-door promotion activities on improving ITN utilization found no differences between the intervention and control areas. These results suggest that door-to-door visits to promote ITN hang-up and use may only be cost-effective and promote significant increases in mosquito net use in certain settings, such as in communities without an established ITN culture.

TUBERCULOSIS

BACKGROUND

Tuberculosis (TB), an infectious airborne disease caused by the bacillus *Mycobacterium tuberculosis*, remains a major global health problem. The World Health Organization (WHO) Global Tuberculosis Report indicates that there were 8.7 million incident TB cases and 1.3 million TB-related deaths in 2012, with most of the new TB cases occurring in Asia (59 percent) and Africa (26 percent). Across the globe, TB is strongly associated with poverty and poor living conditions. In recent years, TB incidence has declined by approximately 2 percent per year, with a rate of decline of 2.2 per year between 2010 and 2011; however, this rate of decline is insufficient to reach the global target of fewer than 1 TB case per 1 million population per year by 2050.

Despite the availability of effective regimens and efficient strategies to deliver treatment, TB control worldwide is impeded by two major issues: the emergence of TB-HIV co-infection and multidrug-resistant TB (MDR-TB). Conditions that weaken immune systems, particularly HIV and AIDS, provide

that can shorten treatment courses, including the treatment course for MDR-TB, and can be taken in conjunction with antiretroviral drugs for HIV.

USAID is investing in research activities that aim at improving the diagnosis of TB, shortening TB treatment, preventing ongoing TB transmission and strengthening delivery of service.

RESEARCH AND INTRODUCTION AREAS

Developing more effective diagnostic tools
Many new diagnostic tools for TB have recently emerged, but their performance in diverse epidemiological settings, health system structures and patient groups remains unclear. Through the TREAT TB project, USAID is supporting the implementation of research to assess new TB diagnosis. By using methodology that goes beyond the traditional accuracy test, the tools' impact on both the health system and the patients can be evaluated.

In 2008, WHO's Stop TB Department issued a recommendation for a rapid diag-

Despite the promising data on LPA test accuracy, a number of questions remain about how to optimally implement it as part of routine health care delivery, how patients benefit overall and how these issues vary in different contexts. Following the release of the WHO recommendation on the use of LPA, USAID began supporting research that identifies the costs associated with LPA tests, the prerequisite health system requirements and the impact on the time between diagnosis and treatment. This research is being done in three countries where the same study model has been adapted to local conditions and national implementation plans.

- In Russia, a study is evaluating the impact of LPA on the time it takes for the identification and treatment of MDR-TB patients in both the civil sector and the penitentiary system.

- In South Africa, researchers are comparing LPA to GeneXpert, a molecular diagnosis tool that can detect TB and resistance to the antibiotic rifampicin in about 2 hours. The researchers seek to determine if using the assay is more cost-effective than GeneXpert for identifying and initiating treatment for MDR-TB.

- In Brazil, a project is implementing and evaluating efficacy and cost-effectiveness of various TB diagnostic options, including GeneXpert and LPA.

USAID is also supporting modeling studies to assess the impact of new diagnostic tools on both TB transmission and health systems. Such models will provide guidance regarding the packages of tools most suitable for different epidemiological settings.

Improved drug regimens
USAID continues to support the implementation of the STREAM study. The aim of this study is to determine whether a standardized 9-month regimen that was used in Bangladesh with excellent treatment outcomes can achieve comparable success with slight modifications in different settings. If shown to be effective, this shortened treatment regimen will have a major impact in reduc-

Time Required for Drug Sensitivity Testing (DST)

LPA	5 hours
GeneXpert	<2 hours
Conventional DST	1-2 Months

optimal potential for TB co-infection. Failure to complete TB treatment or mismanagement of medicine can result in the spread of TB that resists current treatments. These two burdens dramatically hamper the efficacy of widely implemented standardized short-course treatment and, consequently, limit the efforts to fight TB worldwide. TB prevention and care continue to be hindered by the lack of rapid and point-of-care diagnosis tools that can detect TB and MDR-TB in adults and children, particularly for HIV-positive individuals. Moreover, TB control efforts continue to be undermined by the lack of vaccines to prevent new cases and the lack of more effective drugs

nosis test, known as line probe assay (LPA), to detect MDR-TB in high-TB burden, low-income settings. The assay is a molecular (DNA-based) test that simultaneously identifies TB and the most common genetic mutations causing resistance to two antibiotic treatments for TB: rifampicin and isoniazid. This technology can diagnose MDR-TB directly from smear-positive sputum samples, providing results in just 5 hours. When implemented successfully, LPA can substantially reduce the time it takes to diagnose resistance to the two treatments, leading to faster initiation of appropriate second-line drug regimens and reduction in transmission (see graphic above).

BENEFITS OF SHORTENED TB REGIMEN

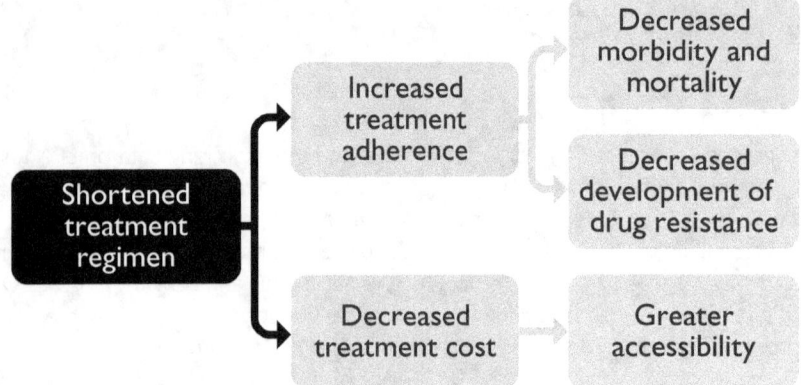

ing the morbidity and mortality of MDR-TB by decreasing treatment cost, increasing accessibility and improving patient adherence (see graphic above). This treatment innovation could also have a catalytic effect in encouraging research and development for new MDR-TB treatment regimens.

USAID is also supporting the evaluation of a number of combination TB treatment regimens with the aim of shortening the treatment of both drug-resistant and -susceptible TB. Data analysis of the first combination treatment was completed. It demonstrated that the three-drug regimen of pyrazinamide, PA-824 and moxifloxacin had the potential to treat both drug-sensitive TB and MDR-TB, thus markedly shortening TB treatment.

A third USAID-supported study is evaluating the early bactericidal activity, safety and tolerability of six new drug combinations in adult patients with newly diagnosed, smear-positive pulmonary TB.

Program performance and management of TB-HIV

USAID has continued to support a number of operational research studies to improve the performance of TB programs by increasing the accessibility of TB services and improving the management of TB-HIV and MDR-TB cases. One exemplary study, carried out through the TB CARE project in Ethiopia, compared TB incidence in two groups of HIV-infected individuals: (1) those who received antiretroviral therapy (ART) for HIV and (2) those who not only received ART but also isoniazid to prevent TB. The study found that TB incidence was significantly lower for the second group. This finding demonstrates the need for all HIV-positive individuals – whether they receive ART or not – to receive isoniazid preventive therapy.

PANDEMIC INFLUENZA AND OTHER EMERGING THREATS

BACKGROUND

The emergence and spread of diseases such as H5N1 avian influenza, severe acute respiratory syndrome (SARS) and the 2009 pandemic H1N1 influenza virus serve as clear reminders of how vulnerable the increasingly interconnected world is to zoonoses – diseases that can be transmitted to humans from animals. Because these diseases can quickly surface and spread, they pose serious concerns to the public health, economic and development sectors.

To protect against the potential consequences associated with emergence of a pandemic threat, comprehensive disease detection and response capacities are needed, especially in locations where threats are most likely to emerge.

USAID's Emerging Pandemic Threats Program seeks to aggressively preempt and combat diseases that could spark future pandemics. Since 2009, USAID has been a leader in supporting surveillance of high-consequence viral families circulating in targeted animal taxa living in Africa, Asia and South America. USAID couples this information with social science research that describes behaviors and practices that evoke viral spillover and spread from animals to humans. In addition, USAID is building the capacity of national workforces to use this information to earlier detect and respond effectively to future threats.

RESEARCH AND INTRODUCTION AREAS

Strengthening surveillance methods
USAID continues to generate new surveillance data on microbes circulating in wildlife populations, with highest priority given to rodent, bat and nonhuman primate species. To date, more than 40,000 animals have been sampled in 20 countries on three continents – South America, Africa and Asia – where new pandemic threats are likely to occur. Using a newly developed set of viral pathogen detection protocols, as well as a global network of laboratories, 250 novel viruses in families known to cause epidemics have been discovered. These protocols are being used to characterize two new pandemic threats: H7N9 avian influenza

and MERS coronavirus. This information feeds into a global database and contributes to mapping microbial distribution and to characterizing the risk associated with different human/animal interactions.

In Brazil, Uganda and Malaysia, a newly launched study is investigating the pathogen diversity across different types of development (urban, peri-urban and undeveloped). This study will help clarify the impact of human activity on wildlife and microbial life and provide insight into how those settings provide new opportunities for animals and humans to share microbes.

USAID is also generating new surveillance data in Bangladesh, China and Vietnam on influenza viruses circulating in farmed animals, including swine, poultry and wild birds. This information will shed light on the distribution, diversity, seasonality and evolution of a family of viruses that has caused four pandemics in the past century. The first round of surveillance took place in the winter of 2012–2013, and samples are being analyzed. A second round of surveillance will take place in the winter of 2013–2014.

Improving the understanding of risk and the role of behavior
In high-risk areas for pandemic threats, often the specific practices of communities and industries, such as the oil, gas and mining sectors, put people at risk. To protect against potential pandemics, it is necessary to

systematically identify high-risk areas and practices, as well as how these activities can be changed.

By re-analyzing the "hotspot" maps of high-risk areas with new datasets, USAID's implementing partners found a stronger relationship between disease emergence risk, human population growth and regions rich in wildlife. New high-resolution risk maps have been produced to provide subnational information on the highest risk areas. These not only show that the underlying drivers of diseases vary by region, but they also indicate that diseases emerge primarily

Emergence of Pandemic Zoonotic Disease

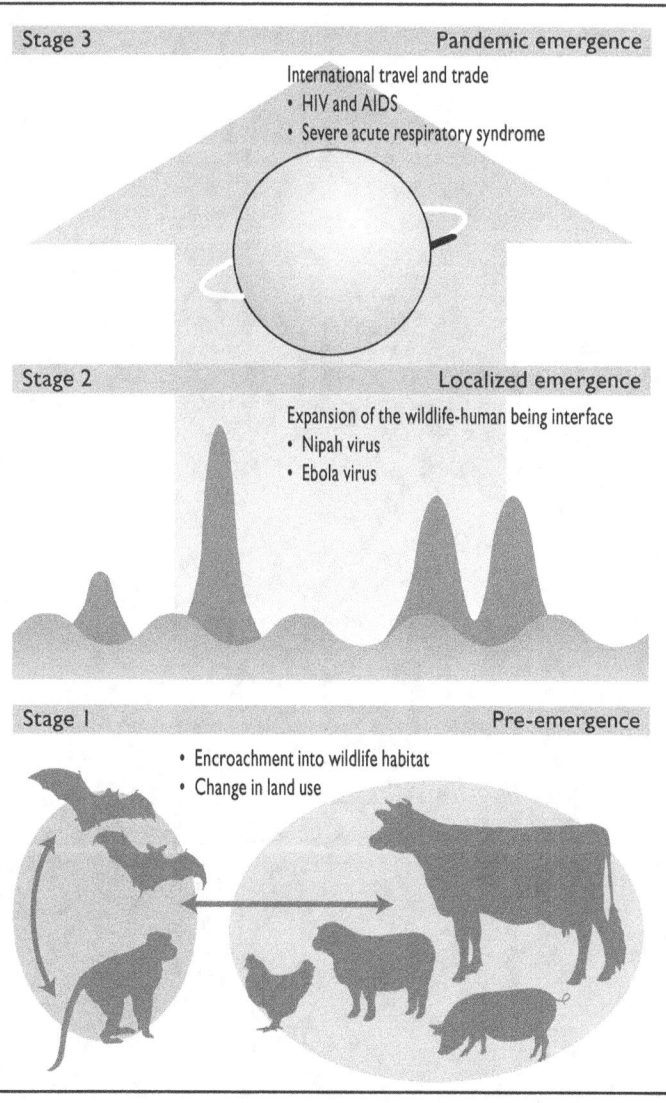

Stage 3 — Pandemic emergence
International travel and trade
• HIV and AIDS
• Severe acute respiratory syndrome

Stage 2 — Localized emergence
Expansion of the wildlife-human being interface
• Nipah virus
• Ebola virus

Stage 1 — Pre-emergence
• Encroachment into wildlife habitat
• Change in land use

This graphic is adapted from S. S. Morse, J. Mazet. M. Woolhouse, C.R. Parrish, D. Carroll, W.B. Karesh, C. Zambrana-Torrelio, W.I. Lipkin, R. Daszak. 2012. Prediction and Prevention of the Next Pandemic Zoonosis. *The Lancet* 380:1956-65.

from land use changes, agricultural intensification and associated secondary factors (e.g., bushmeat hunting and consumption) in locations with the most zoonoses. USAID is assembling the most comprehensive and detailed information available to date on zoonotic disease emergence, using local findings that show high-risk disease transmission from human and domestic animal interactions with wildlife, such as interactions in wildlife hunting, animal crop raiding and wildlife consumption practices. The data collection will guide surveillance, prepare for pandemics and help in the development of disease prevention and control strategies and diagnostics.

Using data from PREDICT, a USAID global surveillance program that forecasts poten-tial diseases in high-risk wildlife, USAID has produced the first-ever scientifically based prediction of the total number of unknown viruses in wildlife mammals. This effort already showed that the number of potential disease-causing viruses (~320,000) is lower than previously suggested. PREDICT global surveillance will continue to provide an estimate of the pool of viruses from which the next pandemic will emerge.

USAID is also conducting in-depth research to locate high-risk populations and identify social preferences, customs and behaviors that are linked with risky contact between humans and animals. For example, USAID projects have mapped poultry trade in Asia and documented wild animal meat preferences of consumers in urban and peri-urban populations in Indonesia, Malaysia, Thailand and Vietnam. This research is being used to develop and test interventions to reduce risk. The project has also developed a generic protocol to comprehensively measure human exposure to animals. This protocol has been tested in northern Thailand and is under way in Lao PDR, Malaysia and Uganda. In Cameroon, USAID has tested an approach to speed up intervention development by rapidly identifying risk-reducing practices and conducting trials to identify which of these changes are most acceptable, feasible and likely to be sustained. A revised version of the intervention will be implemented in Lao PDR and Thailand in 2013.

HEALTH SYSTEMS STRENGTHENING

BACKGROUND

USAID's historic investments in saving lives and improving health around the world have contributed to impressive outcomes. Fewer children are dying from preventable causes. More people are accessing care and treatment for HIV and AIDS. Entire communities are facing a future free from debilitating diseases such as blinding trachoma. For these trends to be sustained and accelerated, and to reach the poorest and most marginalized populations where high mortality rates remain, countries need stronger, more robust health systems that are able to address current and future challenges. However, health system performance in many low- and middle-income countries is challenged by critical health worker shortages, inadequate financing, poor or disjointed information systems and inexperienced leadership.

USAID's Health Systems Strengthening (HSS) strategy builds on proven approaches to address chronic health systems bottlenecks and promotes innovation and research to continually advance state-of-the-art interventions in the six components of health systems: medical products, human resources for health (HRH), information, finance, service delivery and leadership and governance.

USAID's work has shown that health systems strengthening in these areas can improve short-term results and leave a lasting effect. USAID remains committed to HSS to improve the overall quality, cost and accessibility of health care, particularly among the poor and underserved.

RESEARCH AND INTRODUCTION AREAS

USAID's HSS innovation and research portfolio focuses on three main areas:

1. Strengthen and improve health systems performance and contribute to more sustainable programmatic outcomes.
2. Advance methodologies to measure health systems strengthening and performance.
3. Strengthen evidence-based practices for the uptake and use of proven approaches to improve health systems performance and reach at the country level.

Strengthened sustainable health systems

USAID's health systems research examines how to improve health systems performance in a sustainable and country-led way. This includes studies on health worker capacity and retention, health promotion, integration of service delivery and quality improvement methodologies, improvements in costing and cost-effectiveness, innovative health financing and universal coverage and pharmaceutical technologies.

Medical products

Counterfeit medicines are found everywhere in the world, and eliminating them is a public health challenge. Their presence is greatest in regions where regulatory and enforcement systems for medicines are weakest, such as African countries and in parts of Asia and Latin America. With USAID support, a new portable device for detecting counterfeit and substandard medicines is under development. This prototype tool, which is more robust, less expensive and more accurate than current standard technologies, has achieved proof of concept and will be field tested in 2013.

Human resources for health

Support to health workers is essential to ensuring the quality of the services they provide, but more evidence is needed on which types of support are optimal and feasible for retaining a high-quality health workforce. There is a critical shortage of health workers in many countries, especially in Africa. Qualitative studies in multiple African countries will yield evidence that can be used in developing guidance for policymakers and managers on a range of options for improving health worker performance, distribution and retention and for ensuring the delivery of quality care. USAID-funded studies are examining demand- and supply-side mechanisms to support, motivate and hold health workers accountable. A comparative health worker wage analysis in multiple countries will help policymakers adapt wage policies to improve health worker retention.

Evidence is needed on how to increase access to family planning and reproductive health services in underserved areas without compromising quality. A promising approach is to transfer certain tasks from higher-skilled to lower-skilled health workers. Research is under way on task shifting in family planning and reproductive health services to lower-level providers in underserved areas in Zambia, Nigeria and Ethiopia. This work will support improvements in training and in the evidence base for curricula and health care delivery policies.

Finance

USAID supports studies to develop new ways in estimating costs and planning finances for health services. Such tools will help managers and policymakers accurately budget and allocate resources in multiple countries. New methods for costing HIV and AIDS services are being tested. Costed implementation plans are in development. Other studies under way involve the cost dimensions of HIV and AIDS, maternal and child health, family planning and reproductive health and general health services. Costing models that have been developed are being used to improve allocative efficiencies for prevention health services, such as the prevention of mother-to-child transmission of HIV, voluntary medical male circumcision and HIV pediatric treatment, as well as essential health and safe motherhood services.

Service delivery

To better respond to the needs of people living with HIV and to prevent further transmission, prevention-focused research is drawing insight from interviews with individuals on the support they need to reduce their risk of transmitting HIV. The study identifies opportunities for policy, program development and health communication.

Methods to measure and monitor health status and systems

Country governments need accurate information about the status and functioning of their health systems in order to make informed decisions about policies and management. USAID is supporting improvements in HSS tracking and reporting systems, including the development and improvement of indicators and methodologies for data collection that can be used globally. Key progress and results are:

- Continued progress in the development of a HRH Effort Index in order to improve the measurement of and ability to monitor the strength of a country's HRH program. The HRH Effort Index will enable countries, program implementers and donors to more readily assess and measure national HRH program inputs and potentially use this index as a predictor of service use, service quality and health outcomes.

- Improved guidance on measurement and indicators and global leadership to support evidence in national planning for universal health coverage (UHC) and resource tracking. Outputs include evidence-based guidance to help users analyze the efficiency and sustainability of key issues, which will improve the rollout of UHC plans.

- Assessment of essential packages of services (a limited list of public health and clinical services that will be provided at primary and/or secondary care level) in USAID priority countries and development of national guidelines and best practices for transparent and accountable government processes.

- Completion of a survey tool to measure stigma and discrimination in health care facilities. The survey tool supports improved quality, access and utilization of health services by marginalized groups.

- Completion of the development of a module on household health expenditures for the Demographic and Health Survey. This serves as a substitute for more expensive stand-alone survey

approaches. USAID and the World Health Organization will collaborate to field test improvements to quality of care surveys.

- Evaluation of standardized indicators, tools and methods to assess and evaluate performance of routine health information systems.

Scaling up evidence-based interventions
USAID is supporting the advancement of global health systems research priorities, investments in local research capacity and the dissemination of evidence-based research approaches. USAID is evaluating approaches to HSS knowledge transfer, translation and utilization, including efforts to institutionalize change at the country level. USAID supports the development of Health Systems Global, which is the first international membership organization fully dedicated to promoting health systems research and knowledge translation.

To advance the evidence base on how leadership and governance can most effectively strengthen health systems, a literature review of global research explored the link between leadership development, financial management, strategic planning, performance improvement and other interventions that have resulted in strengthened health systems and, ultimately, in better health outcomes for target populations. The findings and recommendations from the review will be forthcoming.

USAID is also advancing the use of modeling tools, which use data to analyze then forecast outcomes of health program designs, for use by ministries of health to plan and govern health systems more effectively. These are needed in many low- and middle-income countries, where governance of health systems has been decentralized, often without sufficient attention to building the capacity and skills of these governing bodies to take on these new responsibilities. A suite of resources is being piloted for the governing bodies of District and Provincial Health Advisory Committees/Councils in Afghanistan, which

have divided the country into 34 provinces with many districts and communities. These resources have the potential to be used in other countries facing similar challenges. Another tool under development assesses national pharmaceutical financing schemes and identifies opportunities for cost savings and improved efficiencies, or alternatively, for financing health services to reduce out-of-pocket expenditures. This tool will help address health system issues that serve as barriers to accessing medicines. It is intended to support policymakers, planners and senior managers in making informed decisions on critical pharmaceutical services.

USAID is strengthening the evidence base for institutionalizing, scaling up and sustaining health care quality improvement (QI) programs through research in Kenya, Niger, Uganda, Tanzania, Russia and Guatemala. In these studies, USAID is evaluating the collaborative method for QI, which uses quantitative and qualitative methods to improve the effectiveness, efficiency and safety of health care service delivery processes and systems, as well as the performance of human resources in delivering products and services. The QI approach assists improvement teams from different clinics and hospitals and from different levels of the health system by supporting their collaboration on common aims to improve particular aspects of the system. They share their experiences as they test changes for improvement. High-level health authorities can then spread the successful changes on a wider scale. The USAID studies are demonstrating how local ownership, integration, resources and incentives are critical to effective design and implementation. They also are providing guidance to policymakers and program implementers for institutionalization and sustainability.

Appendix: Core Funding for Target Health Research Goals

HEALTH AREA	HEALTH RESEARCH GOALS	FY 2012 OBLIGATED FUNDS	FY 2013 EXPECTED FUNDS
MATERNAL AND NEWBORN HEALTH[1]	1. Develop and introduce new and improved evidence-based interventions for care during pregnancy and at birth.	$3,113,364.00	$2,560,616.00
	2. Strengthen and standardize high-quality obstetric care for the prevention, management and treatment of fistula.	$630,000.00	$630,000.00
	3. Design, evaluate and introduce evidence-based interventions to reduce newborn morbidity and mortality from birth asphyxia.	$116,534.00	$722,000.00
	4. Develop, test and introduce community-based health interventions to treat and prevent newborn infections.	$1,262,125.00	$1,220,497.00
	5. Develop scalable, cost-effective approaches for integrating maternal and neonatal health services.	$1,643,330.00	$876,825.00
	6. Assess evidence-based approaches to improve the access and utilization of quality maternal, neonatal and child health interventions.	$2,470,543.00	$572,574.00
	7. Develop standardized criteria and effective tools for measuring maternal and perinatal mortality and morbidity.	$370,000.00	$240,000.00
	Total	$9,605,896.00	$6,822,512.00
CHILD HEALTH[1]	1. Support implementation research to inform the uptake of integrated community case management.	$917,872.00	$ 146,271.00
	2. Develop and test cost-effective approaches to decrease the incidence of acute lower respiratory infections due to household air pollution.	$683,447.00	$ 707,747.00
	3. Evaluate interventions to increase the use of efficacious diarrhea treatments.	$100,000.00	$ –
	4. Develop and test scalable approaches to improve drinking water quality and access, use of sanitation and hygiene behaviors.	$269,026.00	$ –
	Total	$1,970,345.00	$854,019.00
NUTRITION	1. Strengthen and expand the evidence base on integrated multisectoral approaches to nutrition outcomes, such as stunting and maternal and child anemia.	$1,400,000.00	$1,500,000.00
	2. Support implementation research for improved diet diversity and quality.	$2,700,000.00	$2,500,000.00
	3. Develop, refine and expand use of state-of-the-art measurement tools for nutrition programs and policies.	$1,800,000.00	$1,500,000.00
	Total	$5,900,000.00	$5,500,000.00
FAMILY PLANNING AND REPRODUCTIVE HEALTH[1]	1. Refine, develop and introduce new contraceptive methods.	$12,691,000.00	$11,630,000.00
	2. Improve and expand access to family planning methods in developing countries.	$18,284,000.00	$10,648,000.00
	3. Develop and introduce effective, scalable service delivery models to increase the healthy timing and spacing of pregnancies.	$562,000.00	$230,000.00
	Total	$31,537,000.00	$22,508,000.00

1 The projected funding levels for FY 2013 are lower than the previous year, reflecting the final year of research studies, which typically requires lower levels of funding. Additionally, initial planning is currently under way for research translation/introduction activities. The actual funding levels for FY 2013 are anticipated to be higher in the subsequent year's report.

HEALTH AREA	HEALTH RESEARCH GOALS	FY 2012 OBLIGATED FUNDS	FY 2013 EXPECTED FUNDS
HIV AND AIDS	1. Develop and introduce microbicides for women to reduce their risk of HIV infection.	$45,000,000.00	$45,000,000.00
	2. Accelerate the development and clinical testing of novel HIV vaccine candidates.	$28,710,000.00	$28,710,000.00
	3. Strengthen the evidence base to improve HIV and AIDS prevention, care and treatment programs.	$16,353,932.00	$17,320,957.00
	Total	$90,063,932.00	$91,030,957.00
MALARIA	1. Develop safe and effective vaccines to reduce morbidity and mortality due to *Plasmodium falciparum*.	$7,100,000.00	$7,100,000.00
	2. Develop effective and affordable medicines for the treatment and prevention of malaria.	$4,000,000.00	$4,000,000.00
	3. Improve malaria control program implementation and impact.	$4,353,947.00	$4,500,000.00
	Total	$15,453,947.00	$15,600,000.00
TUBERCULOSIS	1. Develop diagnostic tools to more effectively detect TB in individuals with and without HIV.	$2,563,973.00	$1,919,351.00
	2. Develop shorter TB regimens that are effective against all forms of TB, can be used with antiretroviral therapy and are suitable for children, affordable and easily managed in resource-limited settings.	$5,793,027.00	$6,644,684.00
	3. Conduct operations research for improving TB program performance and management of TB-HIV co-infection.	$1,233,400.00	$1,350,000.00
	Total	$9,590,400.00	$9,914,035.00
PANDEMIC INFLUENZA AND OTHER EMERGING THREATS	1. Develop and introduce surveillance methods to increase pathogen detection.	$7,000,000.00	$7,700,000.00
	2. Develop and test methods to improve the understanding of risk, including how human behavior contributes to the risk of disease emergence.	$2,325,000.00	$4,400,000.00
	Total	$9,325,000.00	$12,100,000.00
HEALTH SYSTEMS STRENGTHENING[2]	1. Strengthen and improve health systems performance and contribute to more sustainable programmatic outcomes.	$3,794,074.00	$1,404,764.00
	2. Advance methodologies to measure health systems strengthening and performance.	$5,679,000.00	$3,621,000.00
	3. Strengthen evidence-based practices for the uptake and use of proven approaches to improve health systems performance at the country level.	$701,000.00	$500,000.00
	Total	$10,174,074.00	$5,525,764.00
Total Funding		$183,620,594.00	$169,855,286.00

2 While projected FY 2013 funding for designated health systems strengthening as a targeted area is lower than the previous year, as in the case of family planning and reproductive health, maternal and newborn health and child health the actual funding levels may be higher in the subsequent year's report. Health systems-related research relevant to the other health areas is within the other eight budget lines.

www.ingramcontent.com/pod-product-compliance
Lightning Source LLC
Chambersburg PA
CBHW080748290526
45790CB00008B/3374